Sex: Understanding What You Know, What You Want to Know, and What You Have Not Even Thought About

Michael

A friend & "former" noontime basketball buddy plus a great singer/performer. Let's hope that the contents of this book helps in whatever else might be needed Best

Sex: Understanding What You Know, What You Want to Know, and What You Have Not Even Thought About

● ● ●

Knowing about sex

Thomas Landefeld, PhD

ISBN: 1523735368
ISBN 13: 9781523735365

Table Of Contents

Introduction And Background

THE FIRST QUESTION usually asked of any author is, "Why did you decide to write this book?" For me, the answer is multifold, with all aspects being related. First, looking back to my college years when I was deciding what to do upon graduation, I was always frustrated that even as a science and education major, I had been taught so little about sex and hormones throughout my formal education. I always rationalized it on the grounds that sex was such a controversial topic that teachers and parents did not want it discussed in open settings such as a classroom. As a biology major, this made no sense to me. I knew how important hormones were to the human existence, in addition to being responsible for the propagation of the species! As a result, I decided rather than go into the education field to teach and coach, I would continue my education at a higher level with, yes, a focus on reproduction and hormones. Lo and behold, there was a major doctoral program at the University of Wisconsin called the Endocrinology-Reproductive Physiology Program (although not a degree program specifically having to do with sex but certainly one that dealt with the biological aspects associated with sex and reproduction).

As it turns out, I was accepted into that PhD program, and at last I was in an educational program that focused on sex and hormones. As it turns out, time was spent in the initial classes in the program addressing many of the basic tenets about sexual function, some of which should have been taught earlier. This again prompted me to recognize the tremendous gap in our educational system when it comes to sex education. Since the PhD degree is basically a research degree, learning more about sexual function came naturally in the program through hands-on research in the laboratory, investigating the basic regulation of the endocrine and, specifically, the reproductive system.

As a result, upon graduation with a PhD in endocrinology-reproductive physiology, I now had a much better and broader understanding of the reproductive process, actually both professionally and personally; however, at the same time I realized that many people did not have this knowledge, as they were not exposed to the rigors of attaining a PhD in the field. After additional research positions where the emphases were on the mechanisms involved in maintaining the sexual cycle, I chose to concentrate on educating young people like me who did not really get the proper information about sex through the educational process. (This was of course coupled with many who had not received that information at home from parents either who had often not been taught this formally themselves and/or who were hesitant to discuss the topic due to the views and perceptions on sex.) So I started giving lectures on the basics of reproduction (i.e., anatomy, physiology, and everything related) to undergraduates not only at my campus but also at others across the country. Unfortunately, these students were not at the K–12 level: the problem was that most of these students had not been provided the basic information about sex during those years. Thus, even though they lagged behind in knowing what was needed, we were starting somewhere, and that was important. It is also important to point out that these were not sex education classes but rather lectures in courses like human biology, human aging, endocrinology, and health disparities and, as such, were taught as basic information needed as part of the conceptual nature of the course. For example, how does one understand human biology (particularly the processes involved) if one is not familiar with the workings of the system? And in particular, how do we understand the system that is responsible for not only propagation of the species but also those events that maintain the health and enjoyment of the organism?

Thus, although I was well equipped to teach basic sex from my training and education, having a basic handbook on sex for students seemed to be at least a partial answer to assisting the students not only in understanding the course but, far more importantly, teaching them more about sex and also being able to teach their children, parents, other students, friends, etc. This is especially important as our society now has continued to expose everyone constantly to more sexual situations through media, such as commercial ads, TV, Internet, etc. (yes, sex sells!) without many of those who see these really understanding the basics and therefore often the true meaning.

In fact, on several occasions when I would ask students where they learned about sex, the conversations, for the most part, went something like this:

"In school?"

"Not really."

"From your parents?"

"Definitely not."

"From friends and the street?"

"Usually."

As a result, it is any wonder that folks grew up not really knowing some of the real facts that they should? In fact, growing up, I had a personal experience that exemplifies exactly that. As a young person growing up in a small Midwestern town, long before the Internet, my local schools offered no sex education, and my parents were not at all comfortable talking to me or my sister about sex. Thus, I depended upon my more "experienced" peers, who, as it turns out, were not that "experienced"! Well, in one of those conversations, they proceeded to explain to me that Asian women's genitalia was oriented horizontally rather than vertically! Being inexperienced, naïve, uneducated relative to sex, and without reliable sources, of course I had no reason to doubt them. Interestingly, in retrospect and in a town that was definitely *not* ethnically diverse, I guess that I should have asked where the "experienced" guys got their knowledge and experience!

Obviously much of this lack of information is due to changes in the teaching of sex education in our K–12 schools (e.g., recently, an article in *the Atlanta Journal-Constitution* reported that the focus in the current system is on abstinence and, in doing so, really does not address some of the basic facts about sex, sexuality, and the practical aspects of preventing pregnancy and sexually transmitted diseases, including HIV). Moreover, the parents can choose to have their children opt out of the sex education classes! Again, considering the prevalent presence and nature of sex in society today, it often causes young people to see sex regularly in ads on TV and in movies but not truly understand the real workings of the system. As a result, young people are often not fully aware of the possible negative consequences. An additional concern regarding the lack of proper sex education for young people comes from the almost open availability of porn to children (i.e., Internet). Numbers from various studies recently cited in *Make Love, Not Porn* (Gallop 2011) indicate that (1) the average age when a child first views porn online was eleven, (2) the fourth most popular search term by seven year olds and under was "porn," (3) one-third of the children surveyed had accessed porn online by the time that they were ten, and (4) more than 80 percent of children surveyed between the ages of fourteen and sixteen stated that they had regularly accessed hardcore photographs and footage on their home computers, while two-thirds had watched it on their mobile phones. Relative to those numbers, 70 percent of the children surveyed stated that they had *never* been physically intimate with anyone. Of course this means that for them, their first experience and perhaps understanding of sex was what they viewed online! The question to be asked is: Should hardcore porn be the sex education of today, just by default? If so, this would compound the concern that despite sex being a most natural act and that sex is in the public almost everywhere, does the current generation of boys and girls really understand and appreciate sex as it should be valued?

Just as a note, this is not meant to be a negative criticism of pornography; in fact, in Ms. Gallop's book and website (www.MakeLoveNotPorn. com), she states that she is not "antiporn" but is simply pointing out differences between making love and porn, based very much on perceptions that one might take away from watching porn, especially children and other inexperienced individuals. Two excellent examples are the "money shot on the woman's face" and anal sex. From watching porn, these examples would provide perhaps a very different perspective on what is normal and what is not (even though as stated on the website, choices are definitely individual for everyone when it comes to sexual practices). Providing proper education would at least permit individuals to make appropriate and individualized choices.

As a sidebar to the issue of sex education or lack thereof, it has become obvious that teaching sexual health is equally, if not more importantly, an issue needing to be addressed. The World Health Organization (WHO) defines sexual health as "a state of physical, emotional, mental and social well-being in relation to sexuality; not merely the absence of disease, dysfunction or infirmity. Sexual health requires a positive and respectful approach to sexuality and sexual relationships, as well as the possibility of having pleasurable and safe sexual experiences, free of coercion, discrimination, and violence. For sexual health to be attained and maintained, the sexual rights of all persons must be respected, protected and fulfilled." A true change of course means that changes must occur at all levels (e.g., teachings in the health professional schools such as medicine, nursing, etc., as well as the health-care practice by the health professionals and finally to the degree possible in the home).

So it is hoped that this book can help readers understand some basics that will assist them in leading a life where sex can play the type of positive role that it is meant to in making humans healthy and happy. Moreover, they can actually plan more appropriately concerning when to have a family.

The Anatomy

Of course it is not necessary for everyone to know all of the anatomical parts of the system; however, when learning about how the system works, it is important to know the organs involved: these are important points not just to understand how things work but also to understand when they do not work. One of the realizations regarding the importance of this resulted from a basic biology laboratory class I was teaching (i.e., an introductory biology class for nonbiology majors). On the examination covering the reproduction system, there was a question showing the male and female reproductive organs, asking that these be matched with the proper name. Amazingly, although students did reasonably well correctly identifying some of the male parts, many did not know the vagina from the ovary from the uterus. Perhaps this was due to the fact that the major male organs were external and thus visual, while the female organs were primarily internal. Interestingly, even though these students were not biology majors, they were young adults who did not know their own reproductive organs nor those of their peers. As such, it is hard to imagine what they really knew about the workings of the system since the organs and their hormones are the basis for both normal and abnormal function. Moreover, even if the instructor had not been clear in the lectures, and if they were not taught this before coming to college, one would like to think that individuals would want to know this information, even if it meant learning it on their own.

So with that introduction, let's briefly review the parts (reprinted from *Biology* [6th edition] by Campbell and Reece).

Human Female and Male Reproductive Systems

• • •

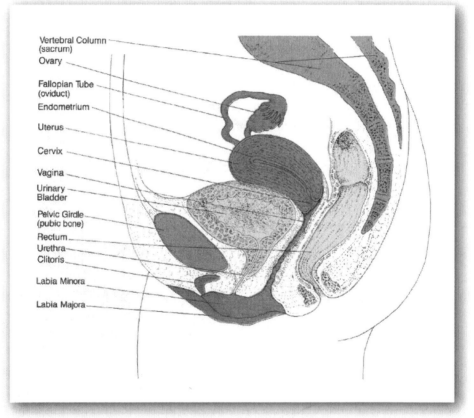

Female Reproductive System

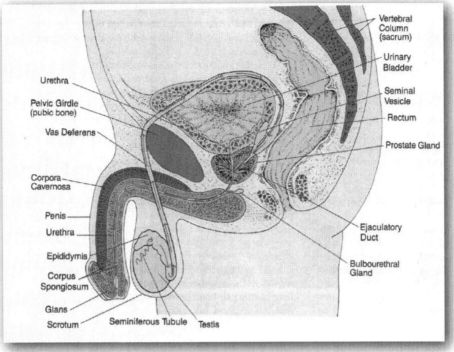

Male Reproductive System

WITH THIS INFORMATION, it is important to further identify the functionality of these organs, as some are strictly for reproductive purposes (i.e., propagation of the species as opposed to sexual purposes, with some serving both capacities).

Reproductive (female)

1) Ovary: responsible for producing and releasing the ova (eggs) as well as key hormones. There are two of these organs.
2) Fallopian tubes: responsible for transport of the egg to the uterus. There are also two of these.
3) Uterus: where the egg, if fertilized, implants for pregnancy, specifically in the endometrium.

4) Cervix: the opening of the uterus from the vagina where sperm can enter and where the fetus moves through to the vagina.
5) Vagina: the opening to the outside where penetration occurs and also from where the baby is born.
6) Labia: the lips (inner and outer) surrounding the opening of the vagina.
7) Clitoris: the structure at the top of the vaginal opening responsible for sensation, covered by a clitoral hood.
8) Urethra: the portal for urination located just below the clitoris.
9) Hymen: the structure within the vagina that characteristically defines virginity.
10) Vulva: the entire external genital area.

Male

a) Prostate: gland responsible for producing components of the semen.
b) Testes: organs responsible for the production of sperm and key male hormones.
c) Epididymis: structure responsible for the maturation of the sperm before moving into the vas deferens.
d) Vas deferens: structure responsible for moving the mature sperm into the ejaculatory duct in preparation for ejaculation.
e) Seminal vesicles: structures within the testes that produce secretions to the semen.
f) Penis: the organ of reproduction and also for urination. It is composed of spongy tissue, as well as the urethra.
g) Urethra: tube that transports urine and semen to the outside.
h) Scrotum: the organ containing the testes.

Of course, identifying the structures, especially those external to the body (i.e., those that are visible) is important; however, equally important, if not more so, is the function that these play in normal and abnormal situations. To fully understand and appreciate this, one also has to recognize the endocrine system. This is the system responsible for the production of hormones throughout the body, some of which overlap significantly with the reproduction system, whereas other components of the endocrine system are involved with glucose maintenance (e.g., insulin from the pancreas and metabolism, thyroxine from the thyroid gland). In fact for those that overlap with the reproductive system, one can classify the organs into endocrine (i.e., hormone-producing) and reproductive (nonhormone producing), even though some are intricately involved in both systems. For the regulation of the endocrine system, one has to start with the brain, which incidentally is the biggest sex organ (!), with the hypothalamus and the pituitary gland being specific components of the brain. These two structures are integral to the workings of the endocrine system and the reproductive system. Moreover, by being part of the brain, the regulation is greatly influenced by whatever the brain sees, feels, smells, etc.

So once the hypothalamus is stimulated, it releases a hormone called gonadotropin-releasing hormone (GnRH) to the pituitary through blood vessels in the pituitary stalk to cause the production and release of the gonadotropins, follicle-stimulating hormone (FSH), and luteinizing hormone (LH). These hormones travel to the gonads via the circulatory system to stimulate the testes in males and the ovaries in females. A very important role in this stimulatory process is to cause the production of gametes (i.e., sperm in men and eggs in women), since these are essential for reproduction to occur. In addition to regulating this system, hormones are produced in the gonads (i.e., estrogen, progesterone, and testosterone) then serve to feed back to the higher brain centers to regulate the system (i.e., referred to as "negative feedback"). Since the reproductive process (and specifically the production of the gametes in both men and women) is cyclic, the acute regulation of the hormones is critical to normal function. In fact, as will be discussed later, the development of the most widely accepted contraceptive (i.e., the birth control pill) was based on manipulating these hormones and their regulatory properties to control conception. Thus, there is no question that endocrine functions and reproductive functions clearly overlap significantly. For example, the ovary produces a number of hormones that are critical to a woman's health (e.g., estrogen, progesterone, and testosterone), thereby making it an endocrine organ that controls the woman's menstrual cycle. However, at the same time, it is responsible for producing and releasing eggs, which of course are essential for reproduction. Granted, from a practical perspective, a woman does not have to know whether her ovaries are endocrine organs or reproductive organs or both; however, when she experiences problems with her cycle or with fertility, she should know that measurement of the hormones relates directly to the functionality of her cycle. As for other reproductive organs, in the case of the uterus and fallopian tubes, for the most part, they do not produce hormones and so are generally not considered endocrine organs. Yet they are certainly essential to reproduction; when conception occurs, the egg is implanted in the wall of the uterus.

Similarly, the vagina does not produce hormones and is not an endocrine organ. Although because it is the first place where sperm (in semen) is deposited on its journey to fertilize the egg, it most definitely is a reproductive organ. As a major reproductive organ, the vagina and its environment has always been a point of discussion. Anatomically, it is composed of stratified epithelial cells, lubricated by glands and, as a result, is self-cleaning. Thus, the use of widely advertised douches is not necessary; in fact, these are often discouraged due to other components they contain. As a result, the vagina does all it can on its own to stay healthy! However, there are times when it becomes unhealthy: when that is the case, there are signs and symptoms (e.g., changes in the color, smell, texture, and quantity of the discharge as well as itching, irritation, and burning). These symptoms can be due to vaginitis, bacterial vaginosis, pelvic inflammatory disease (PID), and various STDs, including HIV. In addition, proper care and attention can contribute most positively to maintaining a healthy vagina (e.g., choice of underwear, diet, partners, Kegel exercises, etc.).

Still another example of a reproductive (sex) organ is the clitoris, whose *sole* function is for pleasure and, as such, is not an endocrine organ, and its role in reproduction is even questionable. Suffice it to say that since it is there for pleasure, it is definitely *a sexual organ*! In addition, it should be recognized that the clitoris in the shape of a wishbone consists of the head (glans) and the body, the latter running alongside both sides of the vagina, thus permitting the organ to be stimulated both directly (i.e., at the glans of the organ) and indirectly through the vagina (i.e., the body). It is believed that it is through the latter mechanism that orgasm can be achieved during intercourse. Just as a footnote, many believe that the glans represents the clitoris in its entirety. During sexual arousal, the clitoris will swell and become erect, facilitating the organ to be stimulated. Other reproductive structures, such as the labia or lips (both majora [outer] and minora [inner]), are considered external organs (i.e., fat-padded folds of skin that do not secrete hormones but are involved visually and tactilely in reproduction). (Interestingly, these structures are very often involved cosmetically as well, as will be discussed in a later chapter.) The cervix is another internal organ that represents the entrance into the uterus from the vagina, therefore playing a critical role in reproduction in that sperm can pass through it into the uterus. Still another internal structure is the hymen, which is a collar of tissue surrounding the vaginal opening and the subject of many sex mythologies. Often it is considered a gauge of virginity, although a torn or broken hymen does not signify true status of a nonvirgin. Despite this, some cultures believe in the myth to the degree that artificial hymens have been developed. Another defined structure of the female genitalia is the vulva, which is actually a collection of external organs/tissues, including the mons, which is that portion covered with pubic hair, the tip (glans) of the clitoris, and the labia. Finally, it is important to mention the G-spot, which is a topic of intense discussion as to its actual existence and role. Anatomically, it is not a totally well-defined structure other than being defined as an erogenous zone of tissue located on the inside front (roof) of the vagina (named after Grafenberg) that is potentially involved in orgasms as well as possibly female ejaculation (more later about orgasms).

For the male, those structures most easily identified are the penis and the testes, which are both external to the body. As for endocrine versus reproductive, the penis does not produce hormones, so it is not endocrine. However, obviously it is very much a reproductive organ (as well as being directly involved in the urinary system). Incidentally, as an aside, much discussion revolves around the size of the penis, with the idea of large genitals going back to Roman times when large genitalia was viewed to be ideal. Interestingly, the average length of the erect penis is five to six inches, and significantly, the size of the penis does not appear to play a major role in satisfactory sexual experiences, including orgasms, either in the male or female. It is important to note that since so much emphasis is placed on the size (length) of the penis, advertisements populate magazines and late-night TV about how to make the penis larger through various mechanisms, including pills (e.g., Extenzee). Recognize that there is no evidence that any of these actually work. One additional aspect of the penis that garners much discussion is circumcision (i.e., the removal of the prepuce), which is commonly referred to as the foreskin. This procedure has a religious basis, a hygienic one, and, perhaps most importantly, a traditional one. Despite many studies and arguments for and against, many choose the procedure based on individual preferences. However, studies have shown that men who are uncircumcised have higher incidences of infections (e.g., urinary tract infections [UTIs]). Relative to the testes, whether or not they are endocrine or reproductive, they definitely produce hormones (e.g., testosterone, estrogen, and progesterone), making them endocrine structures. Yet they are obviously very much involved in reproduction through their role in producing sperm (i.e., analogous to the ovaries producing eggs). Also, similar to the ovaries, the production of sperm in the testes is cyclic in that maturation of sperm takes one to three months as a continual process throughout a man's life. The other internal organs such as the prostate gland, epididymis, vas deferens, and seminal vesicles are all involved in contributing to normal reproduction function, in many cases contributing to the semen in the ejaculate. As an additional note, the scrotum, and therefore the testes, reside outside the man's body, as sperm can be damaged by higher temperatures. Interestingly, there is not a male organ analogous to the clitoris, and that is there only for pleasure, serving no other role.

The bottom line concerning the organs/structures and how they relate to function is meant to provide individuals with the type of general information necessary to know what can be considered normal functions and what are abnormal, even to some extent before seeking medical attention. The best way to recognize these and to become familiar with them is through masturbation. Despite many different viewpoints regarding this, it is perhaps stated best by Betty Dodson, a noted sex therapist, when she said, "Masturbation is the foundation for all of human sexual activity. It's how we first discover our genitals and develop positive sexual sensations by learning how to have orgasms. You must honor this often maligned sexual activity and see it as the most important love affair you'll have throughout a lifetime."

This is by no means an overstatement, since for both males and females often their first sexual experience is masturbation, either by design or sometimes by accident. And although this may not make them familiar with all of their sex parts, it will certainly make them aware of the feeling as associated with orgasm as a culminating event in their sexuality. Hopefully, alongside the process, there indeed will be a natural exploration of the parts that contribute to that explosive feeling!

The Physiology Of The System: How Does It Work?

— • • • —

Considering all of the aforementioned structures and organs, the question is: Why and how does reproduction happen? (Remember, not *all* sex is for reproduction, even though sometimes the terms are used similarly.) The answer to the first part of that question is easy and straightforward: reproduction happens so that the species can continue. As indicated, sex certainly happens even when this is not the planned purpose, and with more and more technological advances, sometimes the physical act of sex is not always necessarily involved, for example in assisted reproductive technologies (ART), in vitro fertilization (IVF), etc.

The following statement is just a fact/figure regarding sex to consider before discussing the process, simply to provide a reference for the frequency and, as such, its importance: *couples have sex an average of sixty-six times a year, which represents sex every six or so days!*

So what is involved? Of course there is sexual behavior, most often initiated by sex drive, or libido. So how do we define "sexual behavior?" Similarly, defining "sex drive" is equally complex. Why is this? Of course, much stems from the definition of "sex" itself (e.g., is it a noun, a verb, an adjective?) Obviously it can be all of these depending on the context. Let's take "sex drive." Unlike drives for food or liquid, which are predicated on the fact that going without them it is not only unpleasant but also is a threat to the survival of the species, this is not the case for sex. Also, interestingly, as opposed to going without food and drink, deprivation of sex does not necessarily increase the sex drive, *nor* does partaking in sex necessarily diminish the sex drive. Also in contrast to food and drink, individuals can actively seek sexual arousal regardless. Thus, in conclusion, no matter how we define sex, sexual drive, and sexual behavior, these are complex topics that interestingly do not necessarily depend upon the intended purpose of reproduction, or just sexual activity. (This is discussed further in the Sexual Behavior section.)

So what happens when sex is for the purpose of reproduction? If the act is indeed happening for reproductive purposes (i.e., the union of the sperm and the egg), it is best to know about the process of reproduction and those structures/functions already mentioned: the "how" (if reproduction is the purpose, when should the act occur), and is there a best time, and what is that based on? To answer these questions, let's examine the "biology of sex" paradigm, which involves the interaction of hormones from specific organs. In the female, these organs include the brain, the pituitary, and the ovaries, resulting in the secretion of hormones and ultimately ovulation, which is the key event in reproduction. The hormones involved are the gonadotropin-releasing hormone (GnRH), which travels to the pituitary to regulate the production and secretion of follicle-stimulating hormone (FSH) and luteinizing hormone (LH), known as the gonadotropins, as they then serve to stimulate the ovaries. This stimulation of the ovaries leads to the development and release of an egg (i.e., ovulation) as well as stimulation of the production of steroid hormones such as estrogen and progesterone. In addition to these hormones contributing to the normal events of the menstrual cycle, they also serve to feedback to the higher brain centers to regulate the system via "negative feedback" mechanism. This occurs on a monthly cyclic basis, which women are aware of due to their periods (i.e., when they menstruate). But how many women actually know what causes that blood flow and why it is monthly? Essentially, eggs are developing and maturing in the ovaries regularly throughout a woman's lifetime, from puberty to menopause, with often one reaching a point to be released into the fallopian tube so as to get fertilized by sperm, usually once per month. However, this is *not* why women bleed; rather, the bleeding is a result of the egg *not* being fertilized and therefore not implanting into the uterine wall, which incidentally has been built up by the action of ovarian hormones (in particular, progesterone) in anticipation of that event of implantation. When neither fertilization nor implantation occurs, the actual bleeding is the sloughing off of that extra tissue that was built up in anticipation of the fertilized egg being implanted. *Thus, when a woman has menses on a regular basis, it is an indication that her reproduction system is working as it should: that is, an egg has been released in a process called ovulation.*

Lack of menstruation means that she is either pregnant or something is not functioning normally as it should, at least for that month. The entire cyclicity of the woman's reproductive system is based on the interplay of the aforementioned hormones from not only the ovaries but also hormones from higher brain centers (e.g., hypothalamus and the pituitary), with the overall goal being pregnancy and thus propagation of the species. In fact, this system is the best-controlled system in the body, using the "axis" of the brain, hypothalamus, pituitary, and ovary, as well as the process being affected simultaneously with any factors that can exert effects on the brain (e.g., smell, sight, feelings, etc.). An excellent example of the role of these other factors on a woman's cyclicity is when a woman's period is delayed because of stress caused by a number of issues, e.g. job- or school-related concerns, relationships, or worry about almost any significant issue in her life. Thus, when one discusses the organs involved in reproduction and sex as above, it is important to realize also the connection of those organs and their functions with the higher brain centers where regulation really begins. There is essentially no difference in the physiological events between when reproduction is the goal versus "just having sex" (other than perhaps protection against pregnancy).

Since reproduction ultimately requires a union of the egg and the sperm, the male component is obviously required. For the male, although there are similarities in the physiological processes, there are also differences. As for similarities, the man's reproductive system involves some of the same organs as the woman's: the brain, the hypothalamus, and the pituitary and the corresponding hormones (GnRH, FSH, LH). The differences are the male organs and their hormones: testosterone, estradiol, and progesterone. Of course, the relative amounts of the hormones differ across the genders, with estrogen and progesterone being the major ones in the female and testosterone in the male. The cyclic nature between the genders will be discussed more later. As indicated earlier, sperm are produced in the testes and eventually expelled through the vas deferens into the urethra in the penis for the process of ejaculation. If reproduction is the goal, the semen would be ejaculated into the vagina of the woman. Does the ejaculation process define a male's reproductive process as "normal"? *No*, not necessarily, as it would only mean that certain components of the system are working but not necessarily the production of sperm. This is opposed to the female, where it has been stated that if a woman has a period, that means that she has released an egg, and for reproductive purposes her system is working. However, for a man to ejaculate semen, which is the fluid that is expelled at that time, it does not mean that his system is functioning for reproductive purposes unless there are sperm in the semen. As it turns out, there are a large number of components in the semen being contributed by those accessory organs/structures as referred to earlier. For example, the prostate gland contributes about 15–30 percent of the volume of the ejaculate, with the testes contributing a small contribution of sperm. The remaining volume of the ejaculate (65–80 percent) comes from the seminal vesicles, with the total volume being about *one half to a full teaspoon*. Thus, it is possible for an ejaculate to appear to be normal, based at least on volume and consistency, but not contain any sperm. Interestingly, the presence of sperm in the ejaculate cannot be confirmed unless the semen sample is examined under a microscope (or, alternatively, if his female partner gets pregnant and they are in a monogamous relationship). So, asking a man if his reproduction system is functioning normally, he could not really say based on the aforementioned criteria: this is, again, not true for a woman, who knows that she is producing eggs as long as she menstruates. A perfect example is when a man has a vasectomy. All of his reproductive activities seem perfectly normal except that his ejaculate contains *no* sperm, as the vas deferens has been severed, which is why in most cases vasectomies have a 100 percent effectiveness rating for contraception. Similarly, this issue becomes significant in a number of cases where fertility/infertility questions arise (i.e., if a woman is not menstruating regularly, then she is not releasing eggs, whereas a man may appear to be functioning normally while not producing sperm). This is just one example of the differences in this area between men and women, with more to be discussed later.

As for the components of the semen, as contributed by these accessory organs, there are a number of proteins, such as albumin and prostate specific antigen (PSA), sugars such as fructose and glucose, as well as polyamines such as spermine. In fact it is spermine from the prostate that gives semen the smell of cleaning products. As for the viscosity of the semen, it can range significantly from watery to quite viscous, at least until it is ejaculated; at this time, due to the PSA, it becomes much more watery in nature, which is believed to facilitate the movement of the sperm. An example of this can be seen when a man ejaculates into a glass, and within thirty minutes the ejaculate becomes much less viscous. As it turns out, this happens even more quickly in the vagina. As an interesting sidelight relative to the potential use of PSA levels in assessing possible signs of prostate cancer, it has been shown that PSA levels measured within twenty-four to twenty-eight hours after a man has ejaculated will show higher levels of PSA in the blood sample! Thus, it is the contributions of the male accessory organs that facilitate the passage of sperm out of the penis and, for the sake of reproduction, into the woman's vagina. Once there, it is a multitude of processes that must occur for the sperm and egg to form a union, including the sperm making their way into the uterus through the cervix and continuing into the fallopian tubes to fertilize the egg. Of course, even then, for a sperm to fertilize an egg, all conditions have to be ideal, as only one sperm can fertilize a single egg. Science is still not certain about every component that makes this happen—not only for a sperm to penetrate the egg but also subsequently for no other sperm to be able to enter and fertilize afterward. The cell membrane of the egg as well as the head of the sperm both have a number of enzymes (proteins) that are capable to interact, allowing the sperm to enter and after that no others.

As for the actual process in males (i.e., spermatogenesis), the production of sperm, like the production of eggs in the ovaries, is a continuous process: it takes two to three months to reach the stage of a mature sperm. However, unlike the process in the female (i.e., menstruation), there is not a single event in the male that signifies the production and release of sperm. In fact, the release of sperm comes at the point of ejaculation, which is, of course, for the purpose of reproduction. (Of course, this result does not always occur, as in the case of masturbation or when contraception is utilized.) As with the female, the hormones produced by the testes (e.g., testosterone) work with those from the hypothalamus (the gonadotropin-releasing hormone [GnRH]), the pituitary gland (follicle-stimulating hormone [FSH]), and luteinizing hormone (LH) to regulate the production of the sperm as well as the ancillary events that are associated with preparing the man for ejaculation. Thus, again, although there are many similarities between men and women in this regard, the male does not, at least outwardly, exhibit a regular cyclicity as seen in a female's monthly cycle. Despite this, there are many who speculate that men do undergo monthly cycles, not characterized by an observable event but rather through feelings such a mood swings, periods of anxiety, horniness, etc. However, without factual documentation, this is still speculation coming from discussions with many individuals, especially females who are in relationships and are convinced of some type of cyclicity in their partners. This represents another difference between sexuality aspects between males and females.

Thus, in summary, the physiological processes involved with sex/reproduction in men and women share a number of similarities while exhibiting distinct differences, all of which contribute to making sex/reproduction what it is—a process that is not only essential to propagation of the species but also one that contributes to a meaningful and healthy life. Certainly knowing something about the basic processes is critical in either or both situations and especially when the processes are not working as they should.

So let's take the scenario regarding the timing of getting pregnant versus not. I have already indicated that usually one egg is released each month during ovulation. Most often based on the development of the follicles in the ovary (i.e., sources of the eggs) under the influences of both the pituitary and ovarian hormones, this occurs around the middle of the twenty-eight-day cycle with day one being the first day of menses. The life of the released egg with regard to being able to be fertilized is twenty-four to forty-eight hours. As such, it is during this time frame that the sperm can fertilize the egg. Similarly the sperm is viable for a similar amount of time once it is ejaculated (although studies have shown that sperm cells can survive inside a woman's body for as long as nine days!). Therefore, if pregnancy is desired, knowing that the survival time of an egg and a sperm are both about two days, and also knowing when ovulation has occurred, are key to the timing of having unprotected sex so as to optimize conception. The difficulty with this, in addition to the conditions not necessarily being just right, is that it is virtually impossible to know exactly when ovulation actually occurs, despite a number of ways to aid in predicting the occurrence. First, the woman needs to have established her timing pattern for menstruation over time, especially if she has a normally occurring cycle, as that can be the initial basis for predicting. Complementary to this, there are other indicators with limited applicability and accuracy, such as the ovulation kits available over the counter in most drugstores. Other methods include taking one's temperature throughout the cycle, assessing the viscosity of the mucosa in the vagina, and even using phone apps based on information entered into phone. Using this information, having sex during a window established around that time will greatly enhance the chances for conception.

If, on the other hand, one wants to avoid pregnancy and is also not using a contraceptive, the process is subject to all of the pitfalls associated with an unwanted pregnancy, which is a significant concern, since about 50 percent of all pregnancies are not planned. Of course, on the other hand, if the couple's goal is pregnancy, they should have sex as often as possible but especially around those times when ovulation is most likely (e.g., the day of ovulation and the five preceding days). However, since conception is not always the primary reason for having sex, a women's sexuality is not strictly regulated by the changes in hormones during the cycle; in fact, the sexual desires exhibited by women are not completely constant during that fertile time. Much of this is probably due to the amounts of estrogen and testosterone present at that time. Interestingly, a study reported in the *Washington Post* suggested that having more sex at *any time* may actually be a boost to fertility by increasing Helper T cells and thereby boosting the immune system (perhaps in advance of pregnancy). Although the study was based on a small sample, it does link the immune and endocrine/reproductive systems, which unquestionably do work together in many ways, including during pregnancy.

So considering the sexual process, let's break it down relative to some of its components. Of course, one can start with the definition and role of sexual behavior and after that, the "often climax" of the process—the orgasm! Then let's discuss how sexual activity relates to one's overall health and how we can manipulate the system to work for us (e.g., contraception followed finally by citing the differences between the processes across genders).

Sexual Behavior?

What about sexual response? It has been described as having four phases: excitement, plateau, orgasm, and resolution. The excitement phase can also be referred to as libido; and although desire exists in both men and women, as already discussed, the source of libido in women is much more difficult to identify even though we know that, as in men, testosterone is intricately involved and is characterized most often by an erection. Certainly, a number of hormones in addition to testosterone can affect desire (libido), and these include oxytocin, prolactin, vasopressin, estradiol, and cortisol, just to name a few. Moreover, part of the difficulty in treating female sexual disorder (e.g., hypoactive sexual desire disorder [HSDD]) relates directly to the uncertainty relating to the source of desire in female sexuality, which is further complicated by the fact that desire (libido) can be a subjective as far as quantitative measurement. Interestingly, although the four phases normally follow a progression, even if desire may not be evident, that does not prevent the other phases from occurring—although in those cases it is far from ideal or even optimal. For example, during the plateau phase, arousal continues for some time, leading into the next phase (orgasm). The role of the brain in these processes is major and not just hormonal amounts but also other aspects, such as attitudes and other considerations about sex and sexual activities. For example, thinking about sex, fantasies, touching, images, culture, religious beliefs, and previous trauma, such as rape or abuse, all can influence desire, both positively and negatively.

As one moves on, relative to sexual behavior, when we then factor in age (and in particular the aging process), the equation really becomes interesting and the subject of intense investigation and publicity due to the increasing age of the population. In fact, because of the latter (i.e., living longer, being healthier, and often being more stable financially), we are now looking at "old age" no longer as a return to the early childhood stages but rather as a "new generation," with very different views and perspectives than previous ones on a number of topics, especially with regard to sex. This is, in turn, reflected in various products, traveling ventures, and, in general, possible new appearances and needs. As it turns out, this new image is not totally as pictured since as the body ages, so do its parts: and as they age, things such as energy (both overall and sexual), appearance, and general abilities change, usually in a negative way. This does not mean that the individuals cannot be themselves anymore; however, it does mean that things are attenuated, therefore forcing adaptation. A good example of this is that nursing homes previously would either not allow or even sometimes outwardly prevent sexual relations/activities among its patients. This has now changed dramatically at most such facilities. Short of that, many older individuals would adapt to fit societies' norms (e.g., live in separate homes but still spend time together). Also it has been seen that individuals will adapt differently with aging depending upon their genders (e.g., the man staying home while the woman works outside of the home). These types of adaptation are not only as they relate to the individual's aging process but also of course how society has viewed, and in many cases wants to continue to view, older individuals and sex. As with so much in life, the adaptations really are individually based, as one size does *not* fit all.

As for specific sexual behavior and aging, the key is for both men and women to adapt to their decreased physical attributes and abilities by very often depending more upon the level of intimacy experienced. Along those lines there has to be a lesser emphasis on the sexual organs and correspondingly orgasms and more on the relationship, per se. Although menopause is discussed often in well-defined ways (much more so than andropause), these events themselves are not necessarily deterrents relative to sexual behavior and eroticism. In fact, in many cases, postmenopausal women speak of a more sexual lifestyle due to the lack of a concern about pregnancy as well as what time of the month she is in. Granted there may be some side effects that may be negative (e.g., less vaginal lubrication), but that is not necessarily a major reason for not being active. Also, as already mentioned, although a man's biological clock is not nearly as well defined as a woman's, there is evidence that it does make a difference in the reproductive arena, both in terms of actual conception as well as the resulting pregnancy/birth. More research will answer additional questions in this area.

Interestingly, almost five hundred years after the initial drawings by Leonardo da Vinci regarding the act of coitus, researchers used MRI images to clarify facts regarding the act. These results showed that the penis is actually bent upward during the act and, as such, has a tendency to press against the back wall of the vagina—which of course is directly opposite to the location of the G-spot on the front wall. Thus, varying the positions for coitus could in fact remarkably change the stimulation, particularly for the woman. Regarding this, many studies, reports, and articles have addressed the question: What is great sex? Most commonly, the answers have focused on techniques, performance measures, and various novelties or novel approaches. Then Kleinplatz et al. (2009) reported in their study that there were eight major components of "great sex" that were consistently mentioned in their survey group. These were the following:

1) *being present and focused*
2) *connection*
3) *intimacy*
4) *communication, verbal and nonverbal*
5) *authenticity, transparency*
6) *transcendence, bliss*
7) *exploration, risk taking*
8) *vulnerability*

Not surprisingly, their conclusions were that performance and technique were generally of secondary importance to these factors, which again were based on the role of the higher brain centers in the sexual process. However, as with any study such as this, the number and types of subjects is always a major consideration, and more such studies will prove valuable.

At the same time, there are specific examples where sexual attractiveness is directly related to both visual features as well as behavior, with differences between men and women. One study showed that women were more attracted to men that they saw the second time (i.e., more familiarity), whereas men were just the opposite: a face was judged more attractive when observed for the first time. Another similar situation in animals, called the *Coolidge effect*, shows that males who have just mated are more likely to mate more promptly again when presented with a novel female. This has been somewhat simulated in a study with young males using an erotic audiotape recording by a female: when the males heard the same tape a second time, there was less sexual arousal. This is referred to as *habituation*, which can also be observed over time with couples in steady relationships (and not due to aging). On a positive side, this can often be offset by introducing novel aspects, such as fantasies. Interestingly, certain fantasies have been correlated to the sexual self-esteem. For example, women who had more rape fantasies had high self-esteem; they also generally had more sexual fantasies, a wider variety of fantasies, and more positive attitudes toward sex. Moreover, in these cases, it appears that these fantasies were really about an openness toward sexuality and not about power/ control or concerns about guilt.

As a final component to this section of sexual behavior, it is significant to address variations, beginning with what some might refer to as fetishes: there are a broad range of fetishes, and of course the appeal of these depends upon individuals. In fact, orgasms can be experienced with stimulation of a body part other than the conventional genitalia. One such example was the case of a woman who experienced orgasmic sensations upon stimulation of her foot following neurological damage during an intensive-care emergency situation (Waldinger et al 2013). It appeared that this was due to regeneration of sensory nerves to the wrong body regions, especially since the area of the cerebral cortex that maps the foot lies next to the area that maps the genitalia. However, at the same time, feet in normal situations can be a highly erogenous zone, as are other areas that may or may not be considered "traditional" erotic zones (e.g., anus, breasts, nape of neck, back of the knee, etc.). In these cases stimulation can even result in orgasms.

Orgasms!

So how much do we actually talk about orgasms—other than sometimes the question after sex, "Did you cum?" (Which in itself is a most interesting question!) The way that society shies away from discussing sexuality openly is not surprising, except for the fact that sex is a normal part of life, and the orgasm can often represent the culmination of the event. Perhaps one reason for the lack of discussion about orgasms actually relates to two things. First is the real definition (if there is one), and second are the major differences, perceived and maybe real, between men's and women's orgasms. Regarding the latter, we still live very much in a male-dominated society, and when it comes to sex, things are slowly improving. By that I mean that generally sex is about the male experiencing orgasm—not just in adult films but also in real life. For example, how many men are "satisfied" if they did *not* orgasm during the sexual act? Conversely, does the woman expect to orgasm from a sexual experience?

The answer to the first question is very, very few, whereas with regard to the second question, probably not many. In fact, from one study, only 34 percent of men believe that sex without orgasm can be satisfying, as compared to women, 51 percent of whom stated that sex without orgasm could be satisfying. Moreover, men have actually been known to use the term "blue balls" in cases where they have not experienced orgasm as a reason to convince a woman to have sexual activity. (Needless to say that a more simple action could be masturbation!) Now it is dangerous to gener-alize for all of the obvious reasons, especially since individuals are indeed individuals; however, with regard to sex and gender, it is probably accurate to say "not many" to the second question, even in 2015. Another point, although not a major one, is that when a man has an orgasm, it is most often associated with ejaculation, which is obviously visible. But of course for a woman, this is usually not the case. Commercially, again, since many of the early adult film producers were men (and still are) the "money shot" was usually the "climax" of the scene; and whether or not the woman in the video experienced an orgasm was neither here nor there. Relative to that industry, things are changing (slowly), but the "money shot" is still the male ejaculation.

Thus, the basis for much of this discussion has been "historical," exac-erbated by the adult film industry coupled with the history of old-school teaching, which is often passed down from mothers and/or grandmothers. As mentioned, times are changing: there are more women recognizing their sexual independence, especially when one considers (1) the clitoris has twice as many nerve endings as does the head of the penis, (2) the clitoris is present solely for the woman's pleasure, (3) many women can experience multiple orgasms with little (if any) refractory period, (4) in women there are multiple sites that can be stimulated to reach orgasm, and (5) although still somewhat controversial, the existence of the G-spot can facilitate orgasm. As alluded to earlier, much of this stems from a woman knowing her body and what it takes to orgasm (e.g., often through mas-turbation). Certainly males identified this process very early in life and continue to practice it throughout life. Why is it more acceptable in their case, especially when it seems that women reach orgasm through masturbation in a similar amount of time as men? Interestingly, at the same time it has been cited that women, through intercourse, only experience orgasm about a third of the time.

Perhaps it again goes back to expectations and history in that very often a woman may want the closeness/intimacy of a man or even just to feel sexy/wanted instead of reaching an orgasm (or she may want the man to reach orgasm, as that was what she was told sex was about). Additionally, very often she herself does not realize how different each woman is sexually, and as such, not recognizing that the man does not either. In fact, studies have shown that some women may not even be aware that they have experienced orgasms. This goes back again to the goal of sex from the male perspective: if it is important for him to reach orgasm, then however he achieves it is OK regardless of the woman's ability to have an orgasm. As a man, I do believe that this is changing, but certainly not quickly enough.

What about the time needed for orgasm, especially between the genders? Studies report that a man during sex will experience orgasm in four to six minutes, whereas a woman will require ten to twenty minutes. Of course these numbers depend very much on a number of parameters and, as such, only represent generalizations based on studies. Additionally, physiologically, if we look at it from a male perspective, we know that generally, except for young men, multiple orgasms are the exception rather than the rule, as the refractory period dictates this. The refractory period is defined as the period of time (thirty to ninety minutes) that, no matter what the stimulation, the nerves and muscles are incapable of responding to produce another orgasm. As such, men *generally* do not experience multiple orgasms, whereas studies have reported up to 50 percent of women report having multiple orgasms. In addition, some women have reported to experience *serial orgasms*, where a series of orgasms are experienced without a return to the plateau stage in between them.

Interestingly, Masters and Johnson did not clearly differentiate between orgasm and ejaculation, so some uncertainly still exits regarding an "all or none" refractory period in all men. Relative to the discussion above, such a phenomenon could also influence the male to concentrate on his orgasm as the end-all rather than just a step in the process. Conversely, this is even more of a reason why it's so perplexing that more women are not in tune with their bodies when it comes to orgasms, especially considering those points made above. Also, another perspective was provided by Masters and Johnson, stating that the key physiological signs in women (i.e., rhythmic contractions of the muscles around the outer part of the vagina) are the same no matter how the orgasm was triggered, probably the result of direct or indirect stimulation of the clitoris. Other research by Komisaruk and others suggest at least two different types of orgasms (e.g., clitoral and vaginal) with even others possibly being cervical and G-spot.

A process that may or may not be directly connected to female orgasms has been identified but not yet confirmed regarding the details of "female ejaculation": this is referred to—in the media and especially in adult films—as "squirting." Research has shown that the "discharge" can be a few drops or a much larger volume: the low-volume discharge appears to be from the paraurethral glands as opposed to the larger-volume discharge, which is believed to be from the urethra and therefore a form of diluted urine. Regardless, these both can be considered "female ejaculation" even though functionality of the process has yet to be determined. Also, importantly, not all women experience this or even realize they experience it.

What's the answer? The first step in all issues such as this is education: that is, women learning through reading and touching to find out what gives them pleasure. Similarly, men learn through both reading and actual touching what gives pleasure to women, especially recognizing that not all women need the same things. With men and women working together, much can be accomplished!

Medically speaking, addressing libido issues in women is essential to affect change in orgasm frequency. As previously mentioned, the source of a women's libido is much less well defined than that of men and therefore much more difficult to identify and subsequently treat if there is a problem. A prime example would be the fact that until recently (with the "pink

Viagra" pill), there was no medically accepted treatment for low libido in women. And, even with this development, many people, including some scientists and some women's advocacy groups, still question the reliability and effectiveness of this pill. Time and subsequent results will be the true test.

One final note regarding orgasms and, in particular, the differences between men and women. For men, since depositing the sperm into the vagina is *usually* necessary for fertilization to occur, orgasm (or at least ejaculation) is considered essential for reproduction. For women, the orgasm does not seem to have the same effect: that is, having an orgasm has not been shown to have a facilitatory effect in reproduction.

Does Sex Make You Healthier?

The straight answer to this question is *yes*! Of course one caveat is practicing safe sex, but other than that, generally under most circumstances, more sex results in a healthier individual. This of course is for a number of reasons, most relating to increasing physiological and psychological functions as a result of sex. For example, blood flow is stimulated, and with that comes more energy, better function at the cellular and molecular levels, as well as the release of hormones that makes one feel "good" (e.g., oxytocin, endorphins). Also, it has been demonstrated that (1) sex can relieve a headache by releasing tension; in fact, sex is more than ten times more effective as a tranquilizer than Valium; (2) sex is a natural antihistamine combatting asthma and hay fever; (3) migraine and cluster headache discomfort can often be effectively ameliorated via sex/orgasm due to the resultant rush of endorphins; and (4) masturbation can relieve depression. Also, individuals and couples who have sex more often not only live longer but very often look younger for all of those positive physiological changes that occur during sexual activity. In fact, Lewis Terman, a psychologist from Stanford, reported specifically that women who achieve orgasm during intercourse live longer. In a somewhat related manner, researchers have shown a possible antidepressive effect of semen on women, along with a most intriguing possible effect of "swallowing semen" on lowering preeclampsia!

Unquestionably, sex is a physical activity (the basis for the term "sex-ercise"), and calories are burned (e.g., 300–400/hour); however, even with the most vigorous activity, the number of calories burned during the encounter would not represent enough for an effective weight-loss program. Internally, the immune system is greatly strengthened as a result of sex, as evidenced by increased levels of immunoglobulin A (IGA), which has obvious benefits in combatting colds and viruses. In fact, a study by Charnetski demonstrated a 30 percent increase in IGA levels in persons having sex two to three times per week. Relative to major health risks, studies have shown that men engaging in sex at least twice per week were at lower risk of heart attack than those who had sex once per month or less. For men where prostate cancer is a major health concern, it has been shown that men who ejaculated twenty-one times per month were a third less likely to develop prostate cancer than those who ejaculated four to seven times per month. For women, it has been reported that sexual activity can lead to less severe menstrual cramping and, in some cases, shorter menstrual periods. Of course, many of these positive effects result directly from physiological changes specifically with hormones and neurotransmitters (e.g., oxytocin, endorphins, norepinephrine, serotonin, etc.). Of these, much attention has been given recently to oxytocin, specifically with regard to its "bonding properties," as well as for relaxation and stress relief as oxytocin levels are highest at orgasm. Again, all of these effects emphasize the interactions of the many systems in the body, with a major emphasis on the endocrine system and its role in the other systems of the body, including the reproductive system.

I would be remiss leaving this topic without at least mentioning the unhealthy aspects of sex, such as sexually transmitted diseases (STDs), including HIV/AIDS. Suffice it to say that precautions must be taken to minimize these concerns and prevent the transfer of bodily fluids containing the causes of these. This is especially a concern based on the recent findings in the *New York Times* that STDs have shown a recent rise: there has been a 15 percent rise in syphilis infections, a 5 percent rise in gonorrhea cases, and a 3 percent rise in chlamydia cases from 2013 to 2014. There are a number of factors that may contribute to these rises, including the increasing lack of sex education in schools (except for abstinence), as referred to earlier. Finally, although it is not necessarily an unhealthy result, *if* pregnancy is not desired, it can then also be considered a negative effect of the sex act (but preventable with precautions as well), especially when considering that almost one-half of all pregnancies are unplanned.

Contraception

The inverse of infertility is preventing conception. By knowing the physiology of the system, it is then possible to manipulate it so that it serves certain needs. For example, if conception is not desired, the process can be manipulated, commonly referred to as contraception (i.e., against conception). Over the years, many efforts have been directed to accomplishing this safely, efficiently, and affordably. In fact, it has been now over fifty years since the birth control pill was first introduced, even though there were many nonhormonal methods before that, all of them in one way or another preventing the union of the egg and the sperm. Of course, one such method was abstinence, which is the most effective means, although this method means no sex. Another method practiced actually allowed sex and was referred to as the *rhythm method,* where couples depended upon knowing the cycle pattern of the woman in combination with observing the measurement of the woman's temperature and, as such, would abstain from sex during the time when they believed that ovulation was most likely going to occur. Unfortunately, because of the inexact nature of the timing of ovulation, this method was not very effective. Another method that was practiced was withdrawal, which was when the man would withdraw before ejaculation. This method was also plagued with ineffectiveness, as there could be leakage of semen and therefore sperm before ejaculation—commonly referred to as "pre-cum." In fact, at least 40 percent of men have sperm in their pre-cum, and as a result about 40 percent of the cases where withdrawal is used, the presence of sperm can lead to pregnancy.

Beyond these methods were those that depended upon using a barrier, thus preventing the sperm from uniting with the egg. These have included the condom (worn by the male), the diaphragm (worn by the woman), and the cervical cap (woman). Other similar types of methods included the intrauterine device (IUD), which was not totally a barrier method, and the vaginal ring. As is evident, all of these except the condom were used by women. Upon the introduction of the birth control pill (i.e., hormonally based contraception), almost all of the early attempts, up to the twenty-first century, were used specifically and almost exclusively by women using the hormones estrogen and progesterone, and their normal role in negative feedback. The basis of the birth control pill was to prevent ovulation and, of course, if an egg is not released, there can be no conception. The development and advancement of the birth control pills over the years has been phenomenal; the large amounts of the steroid hormones used initially to ensure that pregnancy did not occur have been reduced significantly in today's pills. This does not mean that those who are prescribed the pill should not be cautious, as these are very powerful hormones and need to be used as directed and as best for each individual person. In addition, since there is no need for a barrier, sexually transmitted diseases (STDs) are not prevented, and therefore this danger is a concern no matter how effective the method is for preventing pregnancy.

It is important to note that hormonally based contraceptives for males have not been totally ignored. However, it has only been in more recent years where the prognosis for an effective hormonally based contraceptive for men is most promising. Similar to those for women, this particular contraceptive utilizes a steroid hormone, but in this case it is testosterone rather that estrogen/progesterone. At the same time, a recent report regarding research on rats suggests that a nonhormone protein called calcineurin, which is present in sperm, may offer a possible male contraceptive. Research with other methods in the area of male contraception include intra-vas devices (IVDs), an example of which is Vasalgel, which is a gel injected into the vas defers, whereas another is an herbal medication, gendarussa, which inhibits a key enzyme in sperm. Other possibilities include heat, since heat can negatively affect sperm; adjudin, a drug that blocks spermatogenesis; and retinoic acid blockers, since vitamin A is needed for spermatogenesis. Time will tell, first, whether a male contraceptive will be as effective as the female birth control pill and other methods used by women, and, second, whether society in general will respect and accept it—since it depends upon usage by men. Relative to that, one recent US study indicated that about 50 percent of men would use a hormonal contraceptive if one were available. So, there is hope!

Differences Between Men And Women

Several times earlier in the text, I referred to differences between men and women. Of course, there are obvious anatomical differences between men and women, which is probably the one thing that is known by most everybody, even without formal sex education. However, beyond that, many of both genders are not really aware of the differences, many of which are critical to their sexual functionality and actual dysfunctionality. These have been referred to earlier and will be further delineated here.

> *Thinking about sex*—There are many reasons for differences regarding "thinking about sex" between genders. For example, for women, numerous social and cultural factors play a major role, including the dominance of men in society historically, the role after sex if pregnancy occurs (e.g., men simply passing along their genes, whereas women are burdened with pregnancy and postnatal care), attitudes of peer groups, and, in general, as stated by Dr. E. Perel, "Their desires are more contextual, more subjective, and more layered on a lattice of emotion." Finally, there has been significant discussion about treatment of a woman's low libido, with effective products being extremely limited even now. Although

there have been a number of reasons for this (to be discussed more later), many of these relate directly to the somewhat elusive definition of the source(s) of women's libido.

Cyclicity—Although this phenomenon *may* exist in both genders, it is not only most pronounced in females, but cyclicity is crucial for sexual functionally and reproduction. More detailed scientific investigation of male cyclicity is definitely needed, especially since many of the changes that occur, especially associated with cyclicity events, are at the higher brain centers (e.g., mood swings related to depression or horniness). Certainly, this is impacted by the role that men continue to play in society in the past and today; for example, machismo attitudes do not lend themselves to expressing and/or documenting feelings and emotions. Very few studies have examined this.

Aging—Still another difference between males and females in the sex arena relates to aging, where in women, they reach a stage where their ovaries no longer produce estrogen. This is referred to as *menopause* and usually occurs around the age of fifty to fifty-five. There can be major side effects, since a woman's ovaries have been functional since reaching puberty and especially since estrogen is a most powerful steroid hormone that is involved in many functions in the body in addition to reproduction. For this reason, a number of treatments are available, including the replacement of the hormones, commonly referred to as hormone replacement therapy (HRT), or menopausal replacement therapy (MHT). With the introduction of Premarin for the prevention of osteoporosis, there was a major upswing in HRT treatment for both the effects on osteoporosis as well as suggested protective cardiovascular effects in post-menopausal women. The usage plummeted significantly after the Women's Health Initiative (WHI) reported that there was an increased risk of invasive breast cancer and increases in coronary heart disease as a result of the treatments. Since then, the report has been reinterpreted to indicate that (1) the treatment was not to prevent cardiovascular disease, cognitive decline, or other chronic diseases; (2) the concern regarding breast cancer related more to women who had a history of breast cancer in the family and/or were older; and (3) estrogen alone did not increase the breast cancer risk. As a result, and in combination with more information about the benefits and the risks provided to potential patients as well as continued development of effective hormonal regimens, treatment with HRT is once again, in many cases, considered the treatment of choice. Certainly, as with any treatment, this in itself can have side effects; however, it can offer help with some of the symptoms associated with menopause.

To assist with decision making regarding treatment, recently the North American Menopause Society developed a free mobile app and clinical-decision support tool called MenoPro, with versions for both patients and clinicians.

In recent years, medicine has defined a process in males that referred to andropause. Although testosterone production falls at a rate of about 1 percent every year after the age of thirty in males, testosterone production never ceases as estrogen does in women; in fact, a man continues to produce sperm essentially until he dies. And although aging and the fall in testosterone levels can have effects on stamina, libido, energy, and muscle mass, there is no single defining event in men that truly defines andropause. So asking if an older man has undergone andropause, the answer is usually "I don't know" (if it is not first answered by the question, "What is andropause?"). As such, it is essentially impossible to say definitively whether or not a man has undergone andropause, and as a result, a real difference exists in the reproductive aging process between men and women.

Orgasms. Are orgasms the same in both in the male and the female? Yes and no. Yes, orgasms are usually defined as the culminating event of the sexual act, but they are not all the same within a gender or across genders. For example, what is needed to bring the individual to orgasm can vary significantly within and across genders (e.g., in the female, it is direct stimulation of the clitoris or kissing/fondling of some other part of the body). Interestingly, only a fraction of women reach orgasm just from penetration, and it is believed that those who do experience it (other than by stimulating it directly while being penetrated) do so due to the body of the clitoris, which runs along both sides of the vagina and looks like a wishbone. It is stimulated by the penetration, since the vagina itself is not highly innervated.

At the same time, studies have shown some women can experience orgasm in the total absence of any physical touching of any body part. In the male, usually the penis needs stimulation; however, it could be via the vagina, the hand, the mouth, the anus, or even inanimate objects. What about the phenomenon of being multiorgasmic? Many women are. Most men are not. Does this relate directly to the refractory period that men experience after orgasms that women do not? Or perhaps, as stated, it is because the clitoris solely exists for pleasure. Biologically, why does that difference exist between men and women: that is, the presence of a structure only for pleasure and also the presence of absence of a refractory or recovery period? Is ejaculation in both genders common? Actually, historically, this seemed to be exclusive to males. However, recent evidence possibly involving the G-spot and female prostate suggests that women can ejaculate as well. In fact, this has become a major genre in the porn industry: women who are "squirters." In either case, for both men and women, are orgasm and ejaculation synonymous and simultaneous? Not necessarily! Again historically, and as glamorized in adult films, the "money shot," as it was called, was the male climaxing and ejaculating essentially as one combined process. Even now the adult enter-tainment industry has adapted to showing female ejaculation that appears to be a simultaneous process with orgasm. Sex research-ers have not discounted the female ejaculation, as it is thought to occur; however, the voluminous nature has been said to be more for "selling the product" and in doing so, the concept. Thus, more research on the G-spot, its role, female ejaculation, etc., needs to be done to answer or at least address these questions.

Sexual maturation. In recent years, due to a number of factors, boys and girls are maturing sexually at earlier ages (i.e., girls are developing breasts and starting their periods, while boys exhibit signs of sexual maturity earlier than in years past). Thus, both are developing earlier sexually but with similar processes. One major difference between males and females is the timing of their sexual peak, which for boys is nineteen to twenty, whereas for girls it comes in their twenties or early thirties. Again, biologically, one has to ask: Why does this difference exist? Environmental factors definitely are believed to contribute to the earlier development. Such factors include environmental endocrine disruptors (i.e., EEDs) and hormonal treatments of animals and lifestyle practices, just to name a few possibilities.

Contraception. There still exists more means of contraception, whether they be hormonally based or barriers, for women than for men. Initially much of this was due to more males than females working as researchers; although that is slowly changing, there is a reason we still live in a male-dominated society. Scientifically, the female reproductive cycle is more easily manipulated for contra-ceptive purposes, especially since its cyclic nature is more easily identified. However, since both the sex steroids and the hormones from the hypothalamus/pituitary are similar in both men and women, causing similar physiological functions, more research can hopefully balance the scales in the future with regard to con-traceptive methods.

What About When It Does Not Work?

— • • • —

LET'S NOW DISCUSS some situations where things are not "normal." Generally these can be combined into a category titled "Sexual Dysfunction," with symptoms ranging from slight to moderate to severe. For example, if a female who has a regular cycle of twenty-four to thirty days does not have her period in that time frame, and she is not pregnant as established by abstinence or a pregnancy test, then something is wrong. Granted, it can be transitory and not a serious concern: as mentioned, whatever is going on in her life may delay menstruation by changing the hormonal regimen within the system. If that is the case, usually things return to normal during her next cycle. Whether or not she needs to see a health-care provider depends completely upon her, as it is more than likely that other than getting her history—and it is critical for all women to have some perspective on their menstrual history—the advice would be most likely to wait and see if her next period begins on schedule. If that does not happen, then usually it is advisable to seek out advice from a qualified health-care provider (a physician, PA, nurse, etc.), and preferably one who is familiar with the woman's menstrual history. Obviously there are a number of other issues that can affect a woman's regularity of cycles; however, this venue is not designed to address those, especially since it usually requires seeking an appropriate and qualified health-care provider.

Interestingly, it has been demonstrated that a woman is resistant to talking to even her health-care provider, *unless* the provider asks her specifically about her sex life, which of course causes an underestimation of the number of women suffering from sexual malfunctions; for example, a case where things are not working as they should (which is actually referred to as female sexual dysfunction [FSD]). This can be further divided into other categories, depending upon where the dysfunctions lie in the process. All of these can certainly have an effect on not only the ability to perform (and enjoy) but also the ability to actually reproduce. These categories of FSD range from (1) no interest at all in sex (i.e., little or no sex drive/libido [hypoactive desire disorder (HSD)]), (2) unresponsiveness of the genitals (e.g., failure to lubricate), (3) inability to orgasm regularly (anorgasmia), and (4) too much pain to allow for penetration (i.e., vaginismus). Estimates are that perhaps 30 percent of US women suffer from one or more of these disorders.

Moreover, because of the direct involvement of the brain in the process, primarily through those hormones of the hypothalamus and pituitary, the causes of these dysfunctions can be physical and/or mental and need to be ascertained before treatment is initiated. On the other end of the scale is a disorder referred to as "persistent arousal disorder" or "nymphomania," which is characterized by a woman who is unable to find relief no matter how much sex she has and regardless of whether or not she experiences orgasm. As already discussed, female sexuality is a complex process, and so it is important to identify why this state exists (remember it includes much more than just the genitals—it also includes the higher brain centers). Concomitantly, as such, effectively treating (curing?) the dysfunction is equally if not more complex. This again represents an excellent and unfortunate difference between men and women, which will be obvious when I talk about erectile dysfunction (ED).

Since all of these stages relate in some way to the level of libido in the woman, it makes sense that a generalized treatment would be with whatever messenger is responsible for stimulating libido. It has been established that testosterone is indeed that hormone in both men and women (although most likely not by itself). As such, treating a man with low libido with testosterone generally does not cause dramatic side effects because testosterone is the primary male hormone and, as such, plays other important roles in the male (e.g., muscle tone, energy, etc.). Conversely, in the female, although testosterone appears to be the hormone responsible for sex drive, the amounts for doing so are not well established. Additionally, since testosterone is responsible for masculine features, providing the female with too much testosterone can have a virilizing effect.

Moreover, since very few studies have provided data on the levels of testosterone in women, treatment of women with testosterone to increase their sexual desire can be extremely dangerous. In fact, in 2011 the FDA put female sexual dysfunction on a list of *twenty unmet medical needs* where no safe and effective treatment was available. Since then, following a number of unsuccessful attempts to develop a testosterone patch for women, Libigel, a pill termed the "pink Viagra" (i.e., flibanserin [a.k.a. Addyi]) was recently approved (2015) to treat this dysfunction. Time will tell whether or not this will be an effective way to increase libido in sexually dysfunctional women. However, in the meantime, several precautions have been included in the prescribing of this pill, including the risk of dangerously low blood pressure and fainting, especially if used in combination with alcohol or possibly other prescribed medications, such as antifungals used to treat yeast infections. Moreover, the eventual efficacy of the drug is further complicated by the heretofore unanswered questions: How much desire is normal? What mechanisms should be targeted? The latter is especially relevant since it works to release substances in the brain that have proven to be successful in arousing subjects, as opposed to the ED drugs for men that facilitate getting hard through a blood-flow mechanism, not necessarily linked directly to libido or sex drive. Incidentally, the drug had been disapproved twice before, plus it must be taken daily, as opposed to the ED drugs for men that, except for Cialis, normally are taken before sex. To state again, time and perhaps future research and development will tell if a true libido-stimulating treatment for women can be found!

Although I will not go into detail about other types of female dysfunction (e.g., endometriosis, polycystic ovarian disorder [PCOD], dysmenorrhea, amenorrhea, etc.) suffice it to say that whatever the dysfunction, it relates to something not working in the normal process of developing and releasing an egg, especially on a regular basis, and to interfering with functions (disrupting them) that are needed for the process of fertilization to occur. And, as stated earlier, even if fertilization is not the desired end point, the disruption of the process can still significantly impact the activity (i.e., sex that is needed). However, it is important to mention premenstrual syndrome (PMS) and the more recently described condition premenstrual dysphoric disorder (PMDD). These conditions, particularly PMS, have undergone an interesting metamorphosis over the years. PMS is nothing new, but for many years the medical community did not recognize it as a real medical condition since it only occurred in women and also because it was due to hormonal imbalances during the menstrual cycle. As the view by the medical community changed, over the years PMS did become a diagnosable disorder with criteria established to identify it. Then more recently PMDD was recognized as a severe form of PMS, also with specific symptoms for the purposes of diagnosis and such that the woman's daily functions were significantly disrupted. In addition to the observable symptoms, physical and pelvic examinations are included, as well as a look at one's history of medications to rule out their role and to rule out drug abuse. Also because of the many roles of the endocrine system, hormonal levels are usually assessed (e.g., thyroid hormones). Finally, in many cases of PMDD, coexisting psychiatric disorders have also been found. In both of these situations, it is imperative for the woman to keep a diary of her menstrual cycle regularity. Since the interplay of the hormones during the menstrual cycle is quite complex, and because each woman may have different patterns and outcomes, the treatment for these is not always straightforward. In many cases, not surprisingly, lifestyle changes—including dietary modifications that can result in weight loss, a generally healthier lifestyle, less pressure and stress—all can have a positive effect. However, directly or indirectly, it does involve manipulating the hormone regimens to whatever pattern is normal for each woman.

In the case of the male, there are several issues that can affect both the reproductive and sexual aspects, again many of which overlap. For example, erectile dysfunction (ED), which many know about from the plethora of commercials on TV, is an issue that obviously affects the sexual act and, as such, can impair both reproduction and sexuality. As the name implies, the penis cannot either get erect or stay erect, thereby making intercourse almost impossible. Recent numbers report that as many as thirty to forty million US men are affected by ED. As indicated in the advertisements, there are prescription drugs that can be used to treat this dysfunction and, in most cases, do allow more blood flow to the penis which is responsible for the erectile nature of the organ. Reports are that there are as many as twenty-six drugs available to treat various forms of sexual dysfunction in men, which may seem most appropriate since latest results indicate that about 40 percent of men over forty experience ED, whereas 70 percent of men over seventy do. These medications act within fifteen minutes to an hour after taking them, and the longer-acting ones can actually demonstrate continued effects for twenty-four to thirty-six hours. Besides normal aging, as it turns out, there are several reasons why ED can occur in the male: some of the biggest culprits are depression, certain medications, alcohol, stress, anger, anxiety, self-image, the notorious middle-age spread, general overall health, and, most recently, it has been found that vitamin D deficiency and elevated aldosterone, both of which are part of the endocrine system, can contribute to ED. Although the ED drugs will usually aid in treatment, there are other means for dealing with the disorder, including changing medications that are used for other health issues, adapting a new lifestyle, and dealing with psychological issues. Thus, establishing the cause or etiology of the ED is essential in deciding upon the treatment. Interestingly, even men without signs of ED have been known to take the ED drugs just to enhance their sexual proclivity. As with so many medical treatments, there are a number of concerns when treating ED, even with approved and prescribed drugs such as Viagra, Levitra, and Stendra, which are considered short acting, as well as Cialis (tadalafil), which is longer acting. In addition there are now generic drugs available that have the same effect. For example, since the ED drugs relax the blood vessels and in doing so lower blood pressure, men who have heart problems and are on nitrates should not take ED drugs, as the blood pressure can fall to dangerously low levels. In fact, when Viagra was first introduced, there were some deaths due to the individuals not recognizing this contraindication. Also, since circulation is a major consideration in the use of these drugs, atherosclerosis is a concern, especially since the artery to the penis is very small. In addition, diabetes is also a concern—since the vascular system is involved with this disease as well. On the other hand, a side effect can be priapism, which is a prolonged erection (e.g., four hours or more), which not only is painful but also can result in possible infertility. When taking ED drugs, one must also note that these are prescribed drugs regulated by the FDA. As such, "herbal Viagra" drugs sold without a prescription can be most dangerous, since the actual amounts of the "natural Viagra-type" drugs are unknown. One example was an herbal drug that contained thirty-one times the prescription dose of tadalafil, the active ingredient of Cialis. A report in 2015 noted that there were three hundred herbal products that contained hidden ingredients like those in the prescribed ED drugs. Some have been recalled, but many are still available online, at gas stations, and at other places where individuals can buy them over the counter. There was a well-publicized case involving a former professional basketball player who, after taking such a drug, experienced life-threatening effects. Just as an additional note regarding the ED drugs and their effects, in one study, treatment with Viagra resulted in an improved insulin sensitivity in overweight patients with prediabetes, for both men and women; this is, again, a connection between reproduction and other endocrine-related functions. On the other hand, studies have suggested that some men suffering from ED may be more likely to have a heart attack within a few years, depending of course on the reason for their ED.

As discussed above in the case of the female, there are other reproductive/sexual issues/situations experienced by men that usually require diagnosis and treatment by a health-care provider. For example, males can also suffer from low testosterone levels, since these levels, as previously mentioned, decline about 1 percent every year after the age of thirty to thirty-five. Some common signs of low testosterone levels include thinning hair, loss of bone mass, more body fat, mood changes, confusion/fuzzy thinking, low energy levels, changes in muscle tone, and of course a decrease in libido. Although any combination of these could signal low testosterone levels, a blood test of those levels is critical. Unfortunately, there are several problems in diagnosis: (1) normal levels have a very broad range (e.g., 300–1200 units); (2) much depends on the type of testosterone being measured—for example, free versus bound—as well as the form of testosterone measured (e.g., dihydotestosterone [DHT]); and (3) the fact that men do not routinely have their testosterone levels measured, so if there are changes with regard to symptoms, a blood test will only show the current levels with often no reference to previous levels. Thus, a level of five hundred units may be within the "normal range"; however, that amount may actually be down from much-higher levels before a measurement was done. For this reason, many health-care providers must base their diagnosis of hypogonadism and successful subsequent treatment on the symptoms shown by the patient, especially if they are dramatic. As such, testosterone treatment has been prescribed in recent years at a rate that has alarmed some practitioners and regulatory agencies. Most recently, this treatment was further complicated by studies indicating a possible link between testosterone treatment and cardiovascular incidents. As a result, even more consultation and caution has been used in prescribing testosterone treatment for hypogonadism, especially since more studies are needed to confirm or refute the concerns.

An additional consideration is the fact that many "normal functions" such as exercise, eating, sleeping, and drinking habits, as well as supplemental additives, can all contribute to testosterone levels in the body. For example, maintaining a healthy weight can be most positive in maintaining normal testosterone amounts, especially if this is accomplished by proper exercise and good sleep habits. Moreover, certain foods, such as those high in protein, such as lean beef, chicken, and eggs, as well as fatty fish, such as salmon and tuna, which are high in vitamin D, contribute to normal testosterone levels. Additionally foods rich in zinc, such as oysters, and those high in magnesium (e.g., spinach, nuts) work in the body through mechanisms in the blood to increase testosterone levels. Even one's choice of a morning juice (pomegranate, for instance) can not only serve to increase testosterone levels but also to decrease levels of stress hormones from the endocrine system. Finally, although alcohol is generally often viewed as a stimulant, it is really just the opposite and can lead to lower levels of testosterone.

It is important to note that some men use steroids such as testosterone for bulking up and creating more muscle mass from the anabolic effects of testosterone. This has led to organizations such as the Olympics, professional sports organizations, such as MLB, the NFL, etc., banning the use of these substances due to their performance-enhancing effects. Notably, the amounts of steroid hormones used in these cases are *significantly* higher than those in the cases of treating hypogonadism and actually in the long run have significant deleterious effects on the male reproductive system. Notably, as with all treatments and uses of hormones, the amounts being used have to be carefully monitored. Interestingly, because of the misuse and abuse, an example of another connection with the endocrine system is that human growth hormone (hGH) is now often being used instead of anabolic steroids such as testosterone: it is harder to detect hGH, since it continues to be produced by the endocrine system. As an anabolic substance, it can have similar effects as the androgens and as such must be assessed in similar situations. As a result, the NFL has banned the use of hGH, and a recent report naming several veteran players, including a well-known quarterback, brought the use of hGH to public attention.

At least one other dysfunction in males that receives considerable attention is premature ejaculation. Very often treatment for this dysfunction involves therapy, in addition to any possible physiologically relevant issue.

An important final comment to make regarding any kind of sexual dysfunction in men and women is that there are means readily available for treating dysfunction in men but not women.

Finally, in this section, I will address infertility, since conception and the resulting propagation of the species is for many what sex is really about. Infertility is of course when conception (fertilization) does not occur, and this can be for many reasons. For treatment to be justified, a couple has to have been trying to conceive unsuccessfully for a year. Based on what is known biologically, anatomically, physiologically (and even psychologically), it is not surprising that there may be one of several reasons for this. It is interesting that this has been a problem for many years but never seemed to get the attention that preventing conception received (see next section). The bottom line is that there are many options for infertile couples now available.

There are also fertility clinics that in many cases are rather expensive and also not as helpful as many would like. Still, for couples who want to exhaust all possibilities short of adoption, these clinics are quite popular. Several basic assumptions come into play immediately, the first being age. We know that after menopause a woman no longer releases eggs and as such cannot get pregnant. Additionally, as a woman ages, her eggs are not always as healthy as when she is younger. Obviously that is an important factor for the couples seeking assistance, as well as in the diagnosis by the clinic. As it turns out with men, the question about a "biological clock" interestingly is still not completely answered. For example, there is no question that testosterone levels in males fall after the age of thirty; however, testosterone never disappears, as does the estrogen in women when they reach menopause. As such, men continue to produce sperm essentially until they die. For that reason, in the early days, infertility was almost always attributed to problems with the woman. More recently it has been shown that the male partner is responsible in close to 50 percent of the cases of a couple's infertility, which brings up the question of advanced paternal age and what possible effects that may have.

This most obviously can relate directly to the drop in testosterone, since low testosterone levels have been associated with increases in cardiovascular risk as well as increases in bad cholesterol. When considered along with decreases in libido and worsening erectile function, fertility may be directly affected. It was been shown that older men are less likely to conceive and, if they do, take longer time to do so (probably due to lower and/or lesser-quality sperm). This decrease in male fertility also can also be a factor in pregnancies with higher degrees of miscarriage and stillbirth, or pregnancies that result in a neurological or behavioral disorder. Such data have encouraged many more research studies regarding men's reproductive status/ability; yet that area of research still lags far behind. That certainly does not mean that the issues of infertility in women are easy to determine: besides the release of the egg, there are definitely questions about the quality of the egg, the environment for the fertilization to occur, the compatibility of the sperm and egg, as well as many other factors to consider. One additional comment that relates directly to the role that psychological factors play is that in many cases, after a couple conceived through use of a fertility clinic, the couple are then able to conceive using natural means! These are some of the reasons that the fertility efforts are indeed time consuming and expensive. Interestingly also is that quite often if a couple conceives through assisted methods, the result is multiple births (e.g., twins, triplets, etc.).

At least a couple of additional points that speak to the interplay of the many body systems is recent research suggests that smoking and even secondhand smoke is tied not only to infertility but also to early menopause. Still another recent study suggests that infertile men have a higher risk of other health problems such as diabetes, heart disease, and subsequent substance abuse. As indicated above, reasons for infertility are multifold and, as such, often difficult to specifically identify; however, recent studies may add insights into this reproductive problem.

There are several other factors involved with the sexual process that are often referenced but usually with very little discussion. The following represent a few of these.

Endocrine Disruptors. Changes seen in recent years such as puberty at an earlier age, and changes in a woman's cycle as she relocates or as the community around her changes, can be due to a number of factors. Specific ones that have come to the forefront in recent years have been part of a class of chemicals referred to as Environmental Endocrine Disruptors (EEDs) or Endocrine Disrupting Chemicals (EDCs). These chemicals (e.g., phthalates, bisphenol A [BPA], dioxins, atrazine, etc.) now exist in the environment, such as in household chemicals, foods, and liquids in plastic bottles. It is estimated that 100 percent of the world's population have detectable amounts in their bodies, even though the chemicals did not exist prior to the twentieth century. Perhaps even more disturbing is the fact that since 1975 there has been an increase of about one hundred million cases of EED-related effects in children. Moreover, since these chemicals resemble steroids such as estrogens, their effect on the individual's endocrine functions can be adverse and lead to fertility, diabetes, reproductive cycles, obesity, and cardiovascular disorders. And, since the sex steroids play the critical and crucial role in the reproductive system, all processes associated with that system are subject to scrutiny. Thus, not surprisingly, natural processes such as the onset of puberty as well as the beginning of menopause can definitely be affected by EEDs. In fact, recently, the International Federation of Gynecology and Obstetrics (FIGO) reported that increased exposure to toxic chemicals in the last forty years poses significant threats to human reproduction and health. Moreover, a concern is not just in these chemicals modifying the normal body processes but also of course cancer-contributing to not-so-normal conditions, such as certain types of cancers as well as other abnormal conditions such as menstrual disorders.

Currently, it has not been established what levels of these substances cause the deleterious effects, especially since people are exposed to them almost daily through a number of situations—and in fact it is most likely that the cumulative effects are what prove most harmful. Still, because of their ubiquitous presence, it is almost impossible to avoid them completely and, as such, awareness of them is critical. As a part of this section, it is critical to note that many other substances can also cause problems, and these include monosodium glutamate (MSG), artificial sweeteners (e.g.,

Equal, Splenda, and Sweet and Low), artificial colors, high fructose corn syrup, sodium nitrates and nitrites, as well as butylated hydroxyanisole (BHA), just to name a few. In almost all cases, one of the body's systems subject to the effects of these is the endocrine system. Thus, even if these cannot be eliminated or totally avoided, one must become educated as to the possible dangers of these ingredients—especially since they can indeed negatively affect reproduction and, as such, the propagation of the species.

Pheromones. No discussion of sex would be complete without including the topic of pheromones, which are those substances considered attractants and that play a significant role in the animal kingdom, although their role in human life is still a subject of controversy. Back in 1959 Tristram Wyatt coined the term "pheromone" based on studies done with the female silk moth as well as studies with crustaceans. Certainly since then, studies have been conducted over the years and are still ongoing to identify the role of pheromones in human sexuality—and quite honestly, in some circles for a commercial motive (e.g., perfume/cologne!). In the field of reproductive sciences, it is hard to imagine that these substances have no function in humans, especially since they play such a major role in the reproductive process in other mammalian species (e.g., canines, ovine, etc.). One key question is the anatomical origin of pheromones, which in many mammals is a musk gland, whereas in humans it is believed to be the apocrine sweat gland. Also, of course, part of the difficulty in identifying this in humans could lie in the fact that humans have a tendency to use all kinds of substances to look, feel, and smell more attractive; and although pheromones do not have an odor, they are sensed through vasomotor mechanism. In fact, the key organ involved is the vomeronasal organ (VNO), which is an auxiliary olfactory organ containing sensory neurons that connect to the limbic region of the brain. Generally, the VNO is not found in humans, thus complicating the hypothesis of human pheromones. This is in addition to the earlier mentioned fact that humans use a plethora of substances to enhance their appearance, which further complicates studies trying to identify specific human pheromones. Still, studies are being conducted to establish the human pheromone link, especially since there may be a link between pheromones and the detection of a woman's actual time of ovulation (i.e., since if the reason for sex is reproduction, having sex near the time of ovulation would greatly promote that). For example, in studies, women are more attractive to men with lower voices and/or those with more masculine features near the time that they are ovulating (not surprisingly, if reproduction is the goal). Similarly, studies with exotic dancers have shown that lap dancers earn more monies during the time that they may be ovulating as compared to those other times of the cycle and to those on birth control (i.e., anovulatory).

In the meantime, *indirect* evidence, perhaps (!), has been espoused that since women who live together "cycle together" as a result of their pheromones since no other tangible factors would cause this to happen. Such a study was reported back in 1971 by McClintock. Despite these examples, the question of the role of pheromones in humans remains unanswered.

Still, scientifically, significant studies have been and are being conducted, and as stated, this lack of proven data has not prevented a number of commercial companies from producing and selling products that are professed to be indeed human pheromones, ranging from specific products to additives to soaps and other body washes (e.g., Athena Institute sells Athena X for men and 10:13 for women). It is important to note, and has been discussed earlier, that the center for much of the sexual responses resides in the brain and, as such, are psychological in nature, which in no way means that it is all "in one's head," because the release physiologically of components in the brain can be directly affected by psychological effectors, such as thoughts, feelings, smells, etc. For example, certainly those who believe that they are more attractive due to such an additive are more likely to conduct and carry themselves more confidently and, as such, could actually be seen as more attractive!

Aphrodisiacs. A number of agents have been identified over time as aphrodisiacs (i.e., substances intended to improve sexual desire [increase libido], performance, and/or pleasure)—dating back to ancient Rome. The term "aphrodisiac" is derived from Aphrodite, the goddess of love and sexuality, and was most likely initially based on the smell of one's body, especially before the advent of all of the components such as soap, deodorants, and perfumes that were designed to make humans smell better. Some of these are cultural beliefs, some are legends, and some actually have a scientific basis. Regardless, it is important to remember that *the biggest sex organ is the brain*, which is also the source of many substances: neurotransmitters, signaling chemicals, hormones, as well as the site for thoughts, visual input/analysis, moods, etc.

Some so-called aphrodisiacs used today include Spanish Fly; vitamin E; L-dopa; Quaalude; a number of foods, including oysters, celery, bananas, avocados, almonds, eggs, mangos, figs, and garlic; and a number of herbs, such as Korean ginseng and yohimbe. Why these might have this effect is often based on the ingredients within them. For example, celery contains androsterone, oysters contain zinc and dopamine, bananas contain the bromelain enzyme, garlic is rich in allicin, almonds are rich in essential fatty acids, and figs are high in amino acids. Moreover, in addition to their components, the aphrodisiac nature is attributed to their shape, appearance, and general effect of the way they are eaten (e.g., oysters, bananas, figs, mangoes, and celery). With chocolate, in addition to containing the components theobromine and phenylethylamine, there is the romantic nature associated with chocolate in general. Not surprisingly, certain recreational drugs have found themselves in this category, and although very often they may indeed work, there is the safety factor to consider. Some of these include amyl nitrite (poppers), marijuana, methamphetamine, cocaine, ecstasy, heroin, and of course alcohol. Finally, there are supplements that are not necessarily considered aphrodisiacs but can contribute to a better sex life: these include vitamins A, B, C, and E, zinc, selenium, manganese, essential fatty acids, phytoestrogens, and antioxidants. As already mentioned, a number of these occur naturally in the foods cited earlier. Thus, supplementing one's diet with these is not always necessary to ensure for a good sex life, depending upon a person's regular diet.

In summary, although the components of many of the aphrodisiacs are indeed physiologically significant in the body's arousal mechanisms, commercialization has again crept into society, and one has to be cautious about depending upon products advertised to enhance the libido. These do not represent a quick fix in that arena. Moreover, as also mentioned, since the brain is really the most important sex organ, one has to examine attitudes, beliefs, practices, etc., as part of the solution to adding supplements to enhance one's sex life.

The "Love" or "Cuddling" Hormone? Throughout time, a real definition of love has been elusive most likely because of the complex nature of the topic! Is it emotional, biological, or best defined by society norms? Quite possibly all of these. As scientists, we too have sought the definition and, specifically, as reproductive endocrinologists, looked for the possibility of a "love hormone." Granted, as discussed, many hormones have been identified as major effectors of desire/libido, which, for some, could qualify—but for others, not so much. In recent years a hormone such as oxytocin—not new by any means, but heretofore identified primarily with the physiological roles of parturition and milk ejection in women—has now been identified with new functions. In fact, based on recent studies, it is now being considered the "cuddling hormone," if not the "love hormone." The definition as the cuddling hormone is somewhat directly in line with its known roles in parturition and suckling (i.e., cuddling the newborn). However, the love hormone definition goes beyond that to relationships among adults and even to the possible degree of fidelity. Certainly, based on the degree of infidelity among relationships in the United States, finding a remedy for that is paramount to the sanctity of long-term relationships.

Until recently, causes for infidelity included an unhappy relationship, a moral flaw, or perhaps even a sign of deteriorating social values. As such, treatment often involved therapy. That has not necessarily changed significantly, but now scientists are beginning to look at this problem biologically (i.e., is there a gene, gene expression, or hormones involved?). The main hormones being examined, along with their receptors, are vasopressin and oxytocin. Thus, as with much research, scientists turned to the animal kingdom and in particular to the prairie vole, which exists as two similar species with one major difference (i.e., after mating for twenty-four hours, one species bonds for life [monogamous] while the other is polygamous). As it turns out, the polygamous species has no oxytocin receptors in the brain, *and* also if the monogamous species has its oxytocin receptors blocked, it no longer exhibits the monogamous behavior. With that, researcher Dr. Magon suggested that oxytocin is the chemical of love. Interestingly, there are also high amounts of oxytocin at the time of orgasm in both genders. Unquestionably, there is a bonding component associated with oxytocin in the voles, in the mother/child, and quite possibly also in sexual partners.

Also, interestingly, oxytocin is a component of the drug ecstasy, which causes prosocial and prosexual effects. In fact, Dr. Pfaus suggests, "Anything that makes you feel good is an oxytocin event." Is that a definition also of love? So of great interest is whether it could actually be marketed effectively and therapeutically as a "fidelity drug" (i.e., to prevent infidelity). We do know that monogamy is unusual in nature as humans are among the 3–5 percent of mammalian species to practice it. Moreover, for men, promiscuity has the "benefit" of greater potential for reproductive success, whereas for women that would not necessarily be the case. But sex is not just for procreation (plus, for both genders, cheating can be most pleasurable in activating the brain's reward circuit). So is there justification for a "fidelity treatment" using what we are learning about the biology of the system? Perhaps, at the very least, there may be a need for a drug that could make one soft and cuddly regardless of the circumstances, especially as we as a society seems to be generally moving away from being more empathetic? In addition, as it turns out, there are now studies showing other effects of oxytocin, but with all still relating to the previously alluded to characteristics. For example, what about getting sleepy after sex? Certainly there is a release of oxytocin at orgasm, and it may interact with melatonin, which helps with sleep regulation. However, it appears that more restful sleep comes when the sexual partners are beside each other following sex (e.g., continued bonding?). Other research has suggested a "trust" component of oxytocin actually relating to investing or loaning of money—perhaps a variation of the "bonding?" Still another possible case of trust and social bonding is autism. To these points, oxytocin is often referred to as "the multitasking love hormone." Since oxytocin is released by the pituitary, which is part of the brain, it again emphasizes the role of the higher brain centers in reproduction and sexual activities.

Just as an additional note, as it turns out, another hormone/neurotransmitter released by the pituitary gland is vasopressin, which is known for its effect on the kidney; however, in recent years it has also been speculated to have a possible "fidelity effect" and, interestingly, seems to be highest at orgasm in the male!

Masturbation. Also referred to as "autoerotic behavior." Despite this being essentially a normal, common, and healthy process, because of all the controversy surrounding this topic, it was decided to devote a special section to it, even though it has been referred to several times already. The controversy dates back to Victorian times, when masturbation was considered disgusting, unhealthy, and even sinful, possibly leading to "masturbatory insanity." In fact, the medical community actually bought into this idea. As for society, since it was believed that consumption of rich or highly flavored foods promoted masturbation (while bland food discouraged it), bland foods like graham crackers and Kellogg's cornflakes were introduced and advertised specifically for that reason. It even got to the point where devices were introduced and sold that would actually prevent masturbation. Although the campaign against the evils of masturbation is not as strong as back then, certain groups (e.g., religious groups as well as some parents) still associate negative and guilty feelings with the process. In fact, in the not-too-distant past, comments about masturbation by the US surgeon general ultimately led to her resignation!

In direct contrast to these attitudes and beliefs is the earlier quote by sex researcher Betty Dodson: "You must honor this often maligned sexual activity and see it as the most important love affair you'll have throughout a lifetime."

Like other aspects of sex, there are gender differences with masturbation as well. For example, men are likely to use less diverse means for performing masturbation (usually their hand), whereas women will not only manually stimulate different parts of their genitalia, such as the clitoris, labia, G-spot, as well as other parts of their body (e.g., nipples and breasts) but also possibly with the use of toys such as vibrators, dildos, etc. Moreover, there are other differences, such as the following:

- People over fifty years of age masturbate less than those younger than fifty.
- African Americans masturbate less than other ethnic groups.
- Folks not in a relationship masturbate more than those who are in one.
- People with more education masturbate more than those with less.
- Women with religious beliefs/convictions masturbate less than those who do not have those beliefs, and gays masturbate more than heterosexuals.

Even the time to orgasm through masturbation differs, with men taking from two to three minutes, whereas women may take up to four minutes. As for the possible biological effects, early beliefs based on studies in primates suggested that frequent masturbation rid the organism of "old sperm," therefore increasing the percentage of "newer sperm." Somewhat similarly, it was hypothesized that frequent masturbation could lead to higher quality sperm *but* also lower sperm numbers. These beliefs have not yet been proven scientifically.

Sexual Orientation. What is normal when one refers to sexual orientation? Traditionally, there is no question that it was heterosexual sexual practices. Now, interestingly, this phrase, "sexual orientation," has become almost synonymous with "gender identification." Additionally, although homosexuality has always been practiced, in recent years, gay and lesbian sexual practices have taken more of a role and place in discussions while the country continues to deal legally with gay marriage. Then, even more recently, other sexual orientations have become more prevalent, at least in the discussions about orientation—and of course these are transsexuals (historically) and transgender individuals. As of 2009 "transsexual and gender identity disorder" (GID) was the accepted phrasing. Then in 2013 GID was replaced with "gender dysphoria." Similarly, around that time the term "transsexual" also fell out of popular use. More recently, to be more encompassing, the terms *gender nonconforming* and *gender incongruent* have been accepted. Still, *transgender* continued to be used, as it was not considered to be synonymous with those terms previously mentioned. In fact, the old acronym of GLBT (gay, lesbian, bisexual, and transgender) has now become GLBTQI, which stands for gay, lesbian, bisexual, transgendered, questioning, and intersex, with perhaps even more to be added. As traditional as our country is, and as conservative as it sometimes can be relative to sexuality, developing and using a term that accounts for other types of sexual orientation is a step in the right direction. Of course, unfortunately, this does not mean that there is not opposition to these groups; in fact, I already cited the resistance nationwide to accept gay marriage, punctuated by hate crimes and other violations against individuals who are part of these groups. Thus, we have a long way to go. But the good news is that individuals are identifying themselves and their preferences despite the opposition.

Interesting as well is the fact that individuals who defined themselves as heterosexuals often may admit to gay or lesbian encounters at some points in their lives—although they choose not define themselves as bisexual. Thus, the definition is not always as clear as one might like it to be, often due to society's perceptions/stereotyping/labeling and the resultant implications.

It is important to note that even after all of these years and despite continued research in the area, science has still not answered the question of "nature versus nurture" (i.e., physiological versus psychological).

However, there are a number of known biological parameters involved in the transgender issue, many of which are of course treatments with hormones, with another key component being of course the timing of diagnosis and the possible resultant hormonal treatment. As with almost everything else, still another consideration is the financial aspect. Money does matter, and it matters at all levels, from diagnosis and treatment to the final decisions.

Interesting Facts And Figures

— • • • —

In addition to the lack of knowledge that many have regarding basic sex, there are also many facts and figures that many folks have never even imagined. Granted, these are nice discussion points at parties and other informal gatherings, but appropriately, and not surprisingly, they also relate most directly to the basic facts discussed earlier in this book. The following are a few of these examples:

1) Sex can burn 300–400 calories/hour.
2) For most males, ejaculation, starting from penetration, occurs within 3–5 minutes.
3) On average, worldwide, people have 9 different sex partners in a lifetime, women at 6.9 and men at 10.2.
4) Foreplay in America lasts about 20 minutes.
5) American lovers use only 4.8 positions when having sex.
6) Men produce 1,200 sperm every second, which is 104 million per day and 3.8 billion in a year.
7) The average male penis is 5–6 inches long; a gorilla penis is about 2 inches, and that of a blue whale is about 2.5 meters.
8) The longest erect penis on record was 13 inches, and the smallest was 1 centimeter.
9) The average length (depth) of a human vagina is 4–5 inches.
10) The size of the vagina can decrease by 30 percent as orgasm approaches.
11) During sleep, a 60-year-old man has what amounts to about 9 erections per night.

12) Having sex twice a week can add up to 2 years to one's life while strengthening the body's defenses.

13) A man ejaculates about 7,200 times over a lifetime.

14) A man reaches his sexual peak between 17 and 18 years old.

15) A teaspoon of semen contains about 5 calories.

16) At the point of orgasm, the heart rate in both men and women reaches about 140 beats per minute.

17) The average woman has sex about 3,000 times over the course of her reproductive years.

18) The ejaculate travels at about 28 miles per hour, which is faster than the top sprinter in the 100-meter dash.

19) It takes about 2 tablespoons of blood to make the average penis hard.

20) The testes can increase in size up to 50 percent during sexual arousal.

21) The clitoris contains twice as many nerve endings as does the head of the penis (8,000 versus 4,000).

22) Besides humans, bonobos and dolphins are the only animals that have sex for pleasure.

23) Minute quantities of over 30 substances have been identified in semen.

24) Many women experience a spike in their libido just before their period.

25) Black women are 50 percent more likely than white women to orgasm every time that they have sex.

26) The majority of men under the age of 60 think about sex at least once a day, whereas only about 25 percent of women think of it that often (*WebMD*, Sine 9/5/15).

27) With aging, both genders fantasize less, although men still fantasize almost twice as often.

28) Pubic grooming—almost 90 percent of women between the age of 18 and 24 either partially or totally shave their pubic hair, whereas only approximately 70 percent of women ages 40–49 do.

29) In addition to breasts and genitals swelling during sex, the inner nose swells as well.

30) Most men under the age of 40 can achieve an erection in less than 10 seconds.

31) Forty-three percent of women have experienced heterosexual anal sex.

32) The average sperm can "swim" nearly 7 inches in about an hour.

33) In an average lifetime, a man will ejaculate about 17 liters (~ 1 liter = 1 quart) of semen containing about half a trillion sperm.

34) Sixty percent of men get erect nipples when aroused.

35) The testes increase in size by 50 percent when the man is sexually aroused.

36) During his or her lifetime, the average driver will have sex in his or her car 6 times.

37) Men find women with enlarged pupils more sexually attractive.

38) Sneezes and orgasms are the only two physiological responses that cannot be voluntarily stopped once they have started.

39) The number of wet dreams that a man has is likely in line with the number of years in formal education.

40) White women are more likely to engage in anal sex, particularly if they have college degrees.

41) Women consider penis size the ninth most important feature for a man, whereas men rank it as number three.

42) About one-third of all women over 80 still have sex with their partners.

43) Seventy-five percent of Japanese women own vibrators, compared to the worldwide average being 47 percent.

44) Fifteen percent of people claim to have had sex at work.

45) Fifty percent of single women have sex by the third date.

46) Thirty percent of women who engage in oral sex swallow.

47) Greek couples have sex an average of 138 times per year (highest), whereas Japanese couples have sex just 45 times per year (lowest).

48) Five percent of adults have sex once per day, and 20 percent have sex 3–4 times per week.

49) The adult testicle contains enough sperm to measure a quarter of a mile, if laid out end to end.

Thus, in summary, and as stated early in the book, it is certainly not necessary to know all of the scientific, biological aspects specifically associated with reproduction (many of which are described in the text) *unless* of course one chooses to pursue research or clinical aspects of this scientific area. However, it is important for everyone to grasp the basic and general aspects of reproduction cited throughout the text so that one can use that knowledge to take advantage of those benefits provided by sexual activities as well as avoiding the possible adverse consequences of these activities. Unquestionably, knowledge is power, and probably nowhere is it more important than in this area of the human experience.

References

Andrews, Ryan. "All About Endocrine Disruptors." *PrecisionNutrition.* http://www.precisionnutrition.com/all-about-endocrine-disruptors.

Bakos, S. C. 2008 *The Orgasm Bible.* Beverly, MA: Quiver

Bechtel, S. 1993. *The Practical Encyclopedia of Sex and Health.* Emmaus, PA: Fireside Press.

Blank, J. 1993. *Femalia.* San Francisco: Down There Press.

Block, Jenny. 2015. *O Wow: Discovering Your Ultimate Orgasm.* Jersey City: Cleis Press.

Campbell, N. A., and J. B. Reece. 2002. *Biology,* 6th ed. San Francisco: Benjamin Cummings.

Charnow, Jody A., ed. 2015. "Erectile Dysfunction Risk Linked to Aldosterone." *Renal & Urology News* (November 13). *http://www.renalandurologynews.com/erectile-dysfunction-ed/erectile-dysfunction-risk-linked-to-aldosterone/article/453785/.*

Denney, Nancy, and David Quadagno. 1992. *Human Sexuality* 2nd ed. St. Louis: Mosby Yearbook.

Reinberg, Steven. 2015. "Infertile Men May Have Higher Risk of Heart Disease, Diabetes." *HealthDay.* http://consumer.healthday.com/general-health-information-16/alcohol-abuse-news-12/infertile-men-may-have-higher-odds-for-heart-disease-diabetes-705938.html.

Friedman, R. A. 2015. "Infidelity Lurks in Your Genes." *New York Times* (May 22).

Gallop, C. 2011. *Make Love, Not Porn*. TED Conferences, Graham Hill. YouTube

Gallup, Gordon G., Rebecca L. Burch, and Steven M. Platek. 2011. "Does Semen Have Antidepressant Properties?" *Archives of Sexual Behavior* 31 (June): 289–93.

Online Magazine. 2015. "Vitamin D Deficiency Might Be Tied to Erectile Dysfunctions." *HealthDay*. (November 13). http://consumer.healthday.com/men-s-health-information-24/impotence-news-408/vitamin-d-deficiency-might-be-tied-to-erectile-dysfunction-705226.html.

Herbenick, D., and V. Schick. 2011. *Read My Lips*. Lanham, MD: Rowman and Littlefield.

Horvath, K. 2014. "Homme Improvement: Progress in Erectile Dysfunction Treatments." *Endocrine News* (December).

Joannides, Paul. 2015. *Guide to Getting It On*, 8th ed. Oregon: Goofy Foot Press.

Kaplan, K. 2015. "Scientists Identify Potential Birth Control 'Pill' for Men." *Los Angeles Times* (October 1).

Kohl, J. V., and R. T. Francoeur. 1995. *The Scent of Eros*. New York: Continuum Publishing.

Komisaruk, B. R., C. Beyer-Flores, and B. Whipple. 2006. *The Science of Orgasm*. Baltimore: Johns Hopkins University Press.

Kosfeld, Michael. 2014. "Can Oxytocin Promote Trust and Generosity?" *American Psychological Association* (March). http://www.apa.org/monitor/feb08.canoxy.aspx.

Kristof, Nicholas D. 2012. "How Chemicals Affect Us." *New York Times* (May 2). http://www.nytimes.com/2012/05/03/opinion.

Ladas, A. K., B. Whipple, and J. D. Perry. 1982. *The G Spot and Other Discoveries about Human Sexuality.* New York: Henry Holt.

LaRousse, J., and S. Sade. 2011. *Clitology.* Beverly, MA: Quiver

Leinplatz, P. J., A. D. Menard, M. P. Paquet, et al. 2003. "The Components of Optimal Sexuality: A Portrait of 'Great Sex.'" *Canadian Journal of Human Sexuality* 18: 1–13. http://www.Lustability.com/facts.

Levay, S., and S. Baldwin. 2015. *Discovering Human Sexuality.* Sunderland, MA: Sinauer Associates.

Lowry, Thomas, and Thea Snyder Lowry. 1976. *The Clitoris.* St. Louis: Warren Green.

McClintock, M. K. 1981. "Social Control of the Ovarian Cycle and the Function of Estrous Synchrony." *American Zoology* 21: 243–56.

Magon, Navneet, and Sanjay Kalra. 2014. "The Orgasmic History of Oxytocin: Love, Lust, and Labor." US National Library of Medicine (March 12). http://www.ncbi.nlm.nih.gov/pmc/articles/PMC3183515.

Martin, R. D. 2015. "Oxytocin: The Multitasking Love Hormone." *Psychology Today* (May 12).

Monti-Bloch, L., C. Jennings-White, and D. L. Berliner. 1998. "The Human Vomeronasal System: A Review." *Annals of New York Academy of Sciences* 855: 373–89.

Murphy, L. L., R. S. Cadena, D. Chavez, and J. S. Ferraro. 1998. "Effect of American Ginseng (*Panax Quinquefolium*) on Male Copulatory Behavior in the Rat." *Physiology and Behavior* 64: 445–50.

McNeil, D. 2015. "Spike Seen in Reported Cases of Sexually Transmitted Diseases." *New York Times* (November 18).

Nippoldt, Todd. 2015. "Is Herbal Viagra Safe?" Mayo Clinic. www.mayo-clinic.org/diseases-conditions/erectile-dysfunction 2015.

Norton, A. 2015. "Mouse Study Hints at New 'Male Contraceptive.'" *HealthDay* (October 1).

Pastuszak, Alexander W. 2015. *The Male Biological Clock: Really Bites.* CNN. http://www.cnn.com/2015/11/03/opinions/pastuszak.

Pfaus, Jim. 2014. "Oxytocin Is Double-Edged in Helping Treat Addictions." Oxytocin Central.com (March 12). http://oxytocincentral.com/2011/09/.

Plaud, J. J., and J. R. Martini. 1999. "The Respondent Conditioning of Sexual Male Arousal." *Behavior Modification* 23: 254–68.

Plaud, J. J., G. A. Gaither, S. Amato Henderson, and M. K. Devin. 1997. "The Long-Term Habituation of Sexual Arousal in Human Males: A Crossover Design." *Psychological Record* 47:385–98.

Schultz, W. W., P. van Andel, I. Sabelis, and E. Mooyaart. 1999. "Magnetic Resonance Imaging of Male and Female Genitals during Coitus and Female Sexual Arousal." *BMJ* 319:1596–1600.

Seaborg, Eric. 2015. "The Great Debate." *Endocrine News* (November): 27–30.

Seaman, A. M. 2015. "Smoking, Secondhand Smoke Tied to Infertility and Early Menopause." *Reuters Health* (December 15). http://www.reuters.com/article/us-health-smoking-fertility-idUSKBN0TY32C20151215.

Shabazz, ed. "The Aphrodisiac." *ASIS Assets Magazine* (9).

Shabazz, ed. "Human Body Facts." *ASIS Assets Magazine* (14).

Shabazz, ed. "Reasons Why She Suffers Sexually." *ASIS Assets Magazine* (5).

Shabazz, ed. "Libido and Foods to Enhance." *ASIS Assets Magazine* (3).

Shabazz, ed. "Vitamins for Men and Teens." *ASIS Assets Magazine* (4)

Shabazz, ed. "Foods For a Better Sex Life." *ASIS Assets Magazine* (6).

Thomlinson, Simon. 2015. "The Fake Viagra Tablets That Are Linked to Stroke, Liver Failure, and Even Death." *Daily Mail. www.dailymail.co.uk/news/article-3272206.*

Vann, Madeline. 2011. "Is Sex an Anti-Depressant?" *Everyday Health.* http://www.everydayhealth.com/depression/is-sex-an-antidepressant.aspx.

Waldinger, M. D., G. J. de Lint, A. P. van Gils, F. Masir, E. Lakke, R. S. van Coevorden, and D. H. Schweitzer. 2013. "Foot Orgasm Syndrome: A Case Report in a Woman." *Journal of Sexual Medicine* 10:1926–1934.

Newspaper. 2015. "Here's Why More Sex, Even on 'Off Days,' May up Your Chances of Pregnancy." *Washington Post* (October 7).

Metcalf, Eric. 2015. "Natural Testosterone Boosters." *WebMD* (November 17). www.webmd.com.

Acknowledgements

I AM MOST grateful for the support of my education, both formal and informal, over the years as it has enabled me to learn more every day in the creation of this book. A valuable part of that education came from discussions with my many friends and colleagues. Specifically, I want to thank Nicole Action, Dawn the Self-Esteem Queen, and Karrine Steffans for their assistance in reading and commenting during the writing. I also am most grateful to my wife, Shelia, who not only read and commented on the writing but also contributed in so many supporting and encouraging ways.

Made in the USA
San Bernardino, CA
11 April 2016